How to Pray the Rosary and Get Results

How to Pray the Rosary and Get Results
By Brother Armatus Divino Auxilio
(*also known* as Brother A.D.A.)

ISBN-10: 1542842530
ISBN-13: 978-1542842532

How to Pray the Rosary
And Get Results!

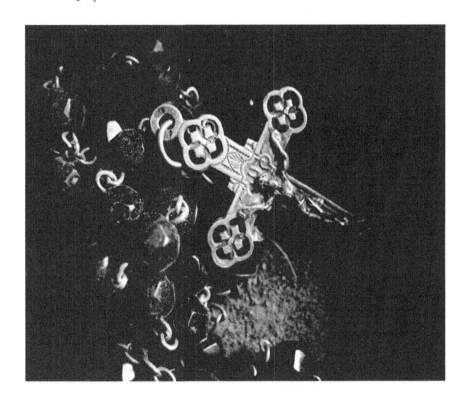

Brother Armatus Divino Auxilio

THAVMA Publications
Dayton, Ohio

About the Author

Originally from Queens, N.Y., and having grown up in Dayton, OH, Brother A.D.A. is a unique figure. He is the product of the unlikely combination of coming from a Traditional Roman Catholic background and a spirituality-friendly home. It was in this home that A.D.A. first learned the basics of meditation, prayer, and spiritual working.

In time Brother A.D.A. completed his theology studies and was ordained to the priesthood and was later consecrated a bishop. He has since left the Traditional movement and brings this knowledge to the "outside world" through his teaching and writing, discussing spiritual issues and practical matters through the lens of traditional Christian theology.

Brother A.D.A.'s coat of arms.
The Motto translates: "Armed by Divine Assistance"

Table of Contents

Pray for us, O Queen of the most holy Rosary.
That we may be made worthy of the promises of Christ.

0. Introduction

The Rosary is one of the most well-known and most beloved devotions in the Catholic Church. Catholics pray the Rosary when they're happy. They pray the Rosary when they're sad. Catholics pray the Rosary when they're afraid. They pray the Rosary when they're mad.

This means nothing is off-limits to the Rosary. It runs the whole gamut of human emotion and human experience. It runs the whole gamut of human spiritual development and human desires. It runs the whole gamut of getting you what you ask for.

As we see in the Rosary a powerful weapon, what does it have that makes it so?

According to one tradition, the Rosary was given by Our Lady to St. Dominic, and Catholic folklore tells us she's appeared at various times throughout history encouraging people to use it. Personally I'm not sure how true those stories are, and the scholarly consensus is that the Rosary didn't gain its modern form until the 16th century.

Either way, there's still something making the Rosary very powerful when used with right focus and intention. In 1998, I used the Rosary to get my love life back together. In 2000, I used the Rosary to get out of a bad situation and get my life back on track. In 2009, I used the Rosary to get a larger-than-expected settlement from a car accident. And so on and so on. In fact, EVERY DAY someone gains benefit from praying the Rosary. Yet for that one person who benefits, there are probably 100 people praying the Rosary and getting nothing at all.

So let's talk about the Rosary for a moment. Let's talk about how you can weaponize your Rosary and make it work for YOU!

"The Rosary is a weapon for these times"
– St. Pio of Pietrelcina

1. What Is the Rosary?

If you ask the average Catholic "What's a Rosary," he or she will likely say it's a string of beads with a crucifix and looks like a necklace. If you ask the average Catholic how to pray the Rosary, he or she may say something like "Apostle's Creed . . . one Our Father . . . ten Hail Marys" and so forth. In essence, the average Catholic will tell you about the *physical dimension* of the Rosary.

What the average Catholic won't tell you is the *spiritual dimension* of the Rosary, either because he or she doesn't know about that dimension, or he or she tried to interact with it and was let down. In fact for all the Catholics uplifted by the Rosary, it's probably safe to say even more find it a chore or a let-down. And it can be a let-down. THE ROSARY IS A LET-DOWN IF YOU AREN'T TAUGHT HOW TO USE IT PROPERLY.

So let's begin our adventure by discussing the physical as well as spiritual characteristics of the Rosary, so that everyone can be on the same page.

History
There are two major theories as to the history of the Rosary, one *mystical* and one *scholarly*.

The mystical theory – espoused by St. Louis de Montfort in his *Secret of the Rosary* – holds that Our Lady gave the Rosary directly to St. Dominic in a vision in 1214, to help Dominic combat the Albigensian heresy that had been rampaging the regions where he was preaching. It's also said that she appeared to Blessed Alan de la Roche, giving him the famous "Fifteen Promises" for all people who pray the Rosary.

The scholarly theory takes a more circumspect approach, tracing the Rosary to the monks' custom of prayerfully reading all 150 Psalms every week. The laity wanted to imitate this practice but were illiterate, leading to a practice of saying the Lord's Prayer 150 times instead, with the prayers being counted using stones or beads. This connection isn't lost on the English language, seeing that our word "bead" comes from the Anglo-Saxon word "bede," meaning "prayer."

Sometime prior to the 12th century, we find people praying the Hail Mary 150 times instead of the Our Father. This is described in a biography of St. Aibert, a Belgian monk who lived from 1060-1140, and, the 1911 *Catholic Encyclopedia* tells us, a monastic rule for anchorite monks in England around the same time.

This custom evolved from here to the 15th century, when in 1569 Pope St. Pius V wrote *Consueverunt Romani*, the first Papal document discussing the Rosary. It remains in fragmentary form today, with the surviving fragment encouraging the faithful to take up the Rosary:

"Following the example of our predecessors, seeing that the Church militant, which God has placed in our hands, in these our times is tossed this way and that by so many heresies, and is grievously troubled troubled and afflicted by so many wars, and by the deprave morals of men, we also raise our eyes, weeping but full of hope, unto that same mountain, whence every aid comes forth, and we encourage

and admonish each member of Christ's faithful to do
likewise in the Lord."

From this point many have written about the Rosary,
its graces, what it can do and has done for them,
and later Popes have expounded on the Rosary and
commended it to the faithful. Most notable of these
is Pope Leo XIII, who wrote no less than twelve
encyclicals on the Rosary.

The most recent papal writing of interest to us is
Pope John Paul II's 2002 encyclical *Rosarium Virginis
Mariae*, in which he gives a "big picture" outline of
the Rosary, describes methods for praying it, and
suggests five additional Mysteries to the traditional
pattern. In the 19th paragraph he specifically states
these new Mysteries are optional – the text literally
translates that these new Mysteries are "left to the
free judgment of individuals and communities."
(*libero singulorum atque communitatum iudicio
relictam*)

Ladies and gentlemen, this concludes our tour of the
history of the Rosary. We now move on to its
physical and spiritual characteristics.

Physical Characteristics
Physically, the Rosary looks much like a beaded
necklace. In fact, many people wear one around
their neck even though it's considered inappropriate.
Others, even more inappropriately, hang one on
their car's rear-view mirror.

The "necklace" had a pendant consisting of a crucifix,
attached to a chain where you'll find one bead, then
three beads in rapid succession, and another bead.

This chain is connected to a "medal," usually with an image of Jesus on one side and Mary on the other, and this medal begins the "necklace" proper. The "necklace" itself has five groups of beads spaced somewhat closely to each other, each separated by one bead spaced further apart.

Sometimes there may be rope or cord instead of chain, sometimes the beads may be metal, wood, plastic, stone, or just knots in a cord, and sometimes the medal may have images other than Jesus or Mary. Some may contain relics inside the medal, while others may have beads made of dried roses (appropriate since the word "Rosary" comes from the Latin *rosarium* or "rose garden").

In its most physical sense, the Rosary is something of a "prayer abacus," a counting tool to help keep track of how many times we've prayed a certain prayer. As our fingers move across the Rosary's beads, we're reminded how far we've come in our devotion for today and how far we've yet to go.

Spiritual Characteristics

While the Rosary's physical characteristics are simple to describe, the spiritual characteristics are much more complex. The short version is that the Rosary's spirituality is contained within 15 "Mysteries" or *tableaux*, each depicting a scene from the life of Jesus and Mary. Each Mystery contains a *spiritual fruit*, or virtue. Each Mystery represents a stage in our spiritual lives. Each Mystery can help us obtain a desired prayer objective.

The 15 Mysteries are contained in three groups of five, called the *Joyful Mysteries*, the *Sorrowful*

Mysteries, and the *Glorious Mysteries*. Here's a complete list:

Joyful Mysteries

These Mysteries are traditionally prayed on Mondays, Thursdays, and Sundays between Advent and the day before Ash Wednesday.
1. The Annunciation
2. The Visitation
3. The Nativity
4. The Presentation
5. The Finding in the Temple

Sorrowful Mysteries

These Mysteries are traditionally prayed on Tuesdays, Fridays, and Sundays between Lent and Holy Saturday.
6. The Agony in the Garden
7. The Scourging at the Pillar
8. The Crowning with Thorns
9. The Carrying of the Cross
10. The Crucifixion

Glorious Mysteries

These Mysteries are traditionally prayed on Wednesdays, Saturdays, and Sundays between Easter and the Saturday before Advent.
11. The Resurrection
12. The Ascension
13. The Descent of the Holy Spirit
14. The Assumption
15. The Coronation

In Protestant Rosaries (particularly the Lutheran Rosary, which we'll be discussing alongside the standard Catholic Rosary), one may commonly find the last two Glorious Mysteries replaced by *The Communion of Saints* and *The Heavenly Jerusalem*. In addition to these traditional 15 Mysteries, there are also the five optional Mysteries added by Pope John Paul II in 2002. These are called the *Luminous Mysteries* or the:

<u>Mysteries of Light</u>
1. The Baptism of the Lord
2. The Wedding at Cana
3. The Proclamation of the Kingdom
4. The Transfiguration
5. The Institution of the Eucharist

When the Luminous Mysteries are added to the Rosary, the scheme for the days of the week also changes. The pattern is as follows:

Monday: Joyful
Tuesday: Sorrowful
Wednesday: Glorious
Thursday: Luminous
Friday: Sorrowful
Saturday: Joyful
Sunday: Glorious

I won't deal any further with the Luminous Mysteries beyond this point, because in my experience it's the 15 traditional Mysteries that contain the core spiritual framework of the Rosary. Many books have been written about these Mysteries and the Rosary as a whole, and of these St. Louis' book is the most outstanding. Yet ultimately, I believe no amount of words can describe all the spiritual characteristics of the Rosary in minute detail, and that to understand the Rosary more fully one must *pray* it. One must *experience* it. One must *engage* it.

2. Basic Method and Rosary Prayers

The method for praying the Rosary is simple, as the Rosary itself is effectively a computational device keeping track of our prayers. As our fingers slide from the Crucifix to the Medal to the single bead to the row of ten beads, we trace a familiar rhythm that's enabled countless people – Saints and sinners alike – to enter into communication with God and tap into their own subconscious. This is a part of what makes the Rosary such a formidable weapon for prayer, because when we sincerely pray it, this rhythm helps us to overcome any distractions the world or even our minds may throw in our way.

How to Say the Rosary

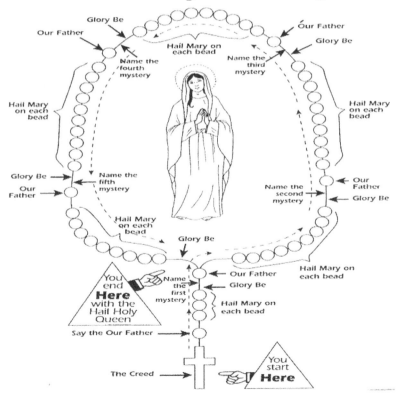

The above image is a guide to the basic method. Now let's discuss the prayers in detail.

1. Sign of the Cross and Apostle's Creed:
Starting at the crucifix, you make the Sign of the Cross:

In the name of the Father, and of the Son, and of the Holy Ghost. Amen.

I'd like to take a moment to talk to my Protestant readers about this, because many think the Sign of the Cross is only "a Catholic thing." No, the sign of the Cross belongs to all who believe Jesus died and rose again for their salvation. So if you believe in Jesus, then the Sign of the Cross is there for you, too.

Afterward, still on the crucifix, you say the Apostle's Creed:

I believe in God, the Father almighty, creator of heaven and earth. I believe in Jesus Christ, God's only Son, our Lord, who was conceived by the Holy Ghost, born of the Virgin Mary, suffered under Pontius Pilate, was crucified, died, and was buried; he descended into hell. On the third day he rose again; he ascended into heaven, he is seated at the right hand of the Father, and he will come to judge the living and the dead. I believe in the Holy Ghost, the holy Catholic Church, the communion of saints, the forgiveness of sins, the resurrection of the body, and the life everlasting. Amen.

The Apostle's Creed is the earliest statement of the Christian faith, considered to be based on a first-century Baptismal formula. It was approved by the original Protestant Reformers and thus accepted by all mainstream denominations, Protestant as well as Catholic, though one may find different wording in different denominations' prayer books. The two most common differences are the word "Christian" used in place of the word "catholic," and the phrase "quick and the dead" in place of "living and the dead."

2. The Lord's Prayer or Our Father

After the crucifix, we find one lone bead, followed by three beads placed close together. On the lone bead, we pray the Our Father:

Our Father, who art in heaven, hallowed be Thy name; Thy kingdom come; Thy will be done on earth as it is in heaven. Give us this day our daily bread; and forgive us our trespasses, as we forgive those who trespass against us; And lead us not into temptation, but deliver us from evil. Amen.

If you're Protestant, you may feel like something's missing. What you're feeling is what I call the "Protestant Ending," because Protestants say it while Catholics don't:
For Thine is the kingdom, and the power, and the glory, forever and ever. Amen.

The reason Catholics don't use this ending is that it's not found in the oldest manuscripts of the New Testament. In fact it's first found in the *Didache*, a Christian document from the late first century:

For thine is the power and the glory for ever and ever.
– Didache 8:10

From here it found its way into the Eastern Orthodox doxology, said after the Lord's Prayer in their Sunday services. The so-called "Protestant Ending" is actually an abbreviated form of this Orthodox doxology:

For Thine is the kingdom and the power and the glory, of the Father and of the Son and of the Holy Spirit, now and forever and to the ages of ages. Amen.
     – from the Divine Liturgy of St. John Chrysostom

In and of itself, there's nothing wrong with adding this ending in your private devotions. If you're praying as part of a group, you may want to ask their stance beforehand so you don't risk falling out of sync with the group, thereby messing up everybody's rhythm (including your own).

Last but not least, there's also what's called the "Debtors' Version" of the Lord's Prayer, where they say "debts" and "debtors" in place of "trespasses." I point this out to make you aware of it, even though people in churches using the Debtors' Version tend not to be interested in a book on the Rosary.

3. The Hail Mary or Angelical Salutation
From the large bead, we move to the three beads strung together. On each bead was say a Hail Mary, one in honor of the Father, one in honor of the Son, and one in honor of the Holy Spirit.

Hail Mary, full of grace, the Lord is with thee; blessed art thou amongst women, and blessed is the fruit of thy womb, Jesus. Holy Mary, Mother of God, pray for us sinners, now and at the hour of our death. Amen.

If you're Protestant, you may have some apprehension with this prayer. Such apprehension is unwarranted, as the original for of the Hail Mary comes directly from Scripture. We find the first phrase in Luke 1:26, with Mary's name added to make it clear who we're talking to:

Hail, full of grace! The Lord is with thee.

These are the words the Archangel Gabriel said to Mary when announcing her role in giving birth to Jesus. So when we pray this part of the Hail Mary, we're simply repeating Gabriel's way of saying "Hello."

The second part of the Hail Mary is found in Luke 1:42, when her cousin Elizabeth salutes her. The name of Jesus is added to the prayer to make it clear who we're talking about.

Blessed art thou among women, and blessed is the fruit of thy womb.

So this is the entire original form of the Hail Mary, all of which is a direct quote from Scripture:

Hail Mary, full of grace, the Lord is with thee; blessed art thou amongst women, and blessed is the fruit of thy womb, Jesus.

This is the form Martin Luther encouraged Christians to pray, as he writes in his personal prayer book in 1522:

*Our prayer should include the Mother of God...What the Hail Mary says is that all glory should be given to God, using these words: "**Hail Mary, full of grace. The Lord is with thee; blessed art thou among women and blessed is the fruit of thy womb, Jesus Christ. Amen!**" You see that these words are not concerned with prayer but purely with giving praise and honor. We can use the Hail Mary as a meditation in which we recite what grace God has given her. Second, we should add a wish that everyone may know and respect her.* (emphasis mine)

In a sermon dated March 11, 1523, he says likewise:

Whoever possesses a good (firm) faith, says the Hail Mary without danger!

This is the foundation on which the Protestant may say the Hail Mary "without danger," because the original form is purely Christological in its context – that is, it holds up and looks through Mary as through a window pointing to Christ.

The other first-generation Reformers – Calvin, Zwingli, and Cranmer – did not favor saying the Hail Mary, though they strongly supported calling Mary the "Mother of God." While this might scandalize later generations of Protestants, it's important to understand their reason was solely Christological: the title "Mother of God" refers to the belief that Jesus is God, and that Mary therefore carried God the Son in her womb.

The last part of the prayer, "Holy Mary, Mother of God, etc." is a later addition dating to immediately before the Reformation. I've always considered it sort of a "Catholic Ending" as it's unique to Catholicism. The only place where this could cause a real issue for a Protestant is in group recitation, where it's common for whoever's leading the devotion to say the first two phrases, and the people all respond by saying this last phrase.

Before closing this section, I'd like to point out that the Eastern Orthodox have their own version of the Hail Mary, based on the same Biblical text:

Mother of God and Virgin, rejoice, Mary full of grace, the Lord is with thee. Blessed art thou amongst women, and blessed is the fruit of thy womb, for thou hast given birth to the Savior of our souls.

As with the Our Father, in private I see no harm in using whatever version you wish throughout your personal devotions. Yet also as with the Our Father, you'll want to find out beforehand which version will be used in a group setting and for very much the same reasons.

4. Glory Be to the Father (Gloria Patri)
On the chain after the three beads, you say the Glory Be to the Father:

Glory be to the Father, and to the Son, and to the Holy Ghost. As it was in the beginning, is now, and ever shall be, world without end. Amen.

This is also called the "Lesser Doxology" and is universally known throughout the mainstream denominations. The Eastern Orthodox have a slightly different wording:

Glory to the Father, and to the Son, and to the Holy Spirit. Both now and always, and unto the ages of ages. Amen.

A person from the so-called "Radical" Protestant traditions will immediately think of something completely different when hearing the word "Doxology," usually sung to a tune named *Old Hundredth*:

Praise God, from whom all blessings flow;
Praise Him, all creatures here below;
Praise Him above, ye heavenly host;
Praise Father, Son, and Holy Ghost. Amen.

I can think of nothing in any of these doxologies that would offend any Christian from any tradition. As with all the other prayers we've discussed thus far, all these options are available when one is praying in private; in group settings, it's best to ask beforehand or just start your own group from scratch.

5. Praying the Mysteries

After saying the Glory Be, we begin meditating on a set of five Mysteries. Don't worry if you don't fully understand the Mysteries, because we'll talk about them in detail in the next chapter.

a. On the bead right after the Glory Be, that's where we begin the first Mystery. On this bead you announce the Mystery, which can be a simple formula or a longer one, whichever you prefer. For example, you could say:

The first Joyful Mystery. The Annunciation.

Or you could go into more detail. As another example, this is the form I use in my personal Rosary practice:

The first Joyous Mystery of the most holy rosary: the Annunciation of the birth of Jesus Christ to the blessed Virgin Mary by the Archangel Gabriel.

The choice is yours in how you want to announce the Rosary. In a group setting, the leader will make this announcement while the rest of the group stays silent; if you're the leader this means you get to choose the words.

b. After announcing the Mystery, you stay on the same bead and pray the Our Father. In a group setting, this is most often done with the leader beginning the prayer, while the rest of the group begins at "Give us this day our daily bread."

c. After the Our Father, you'll notice a medal between this bead and the beginning of the Rosary's "necklace." We ignore that medal for now (it's used at the end of the Rosary), and move to the line of 10 beads right past it.

On these 10 beads we say 10 Hail Mary's, one prayer for each bead. As said before, in a group setting, the most common method is for the leader to begin the prayer while the group starts at "Holy Mary, Mother of God."

d. After the final Hail Mary, we say the Glory Be to the Father. I've seen this happen two ways in group settings: one where the entire group says the whole thing together, and one where the leader starts and the group begins at "As it was in the beginning." ·

e. After the Glory Be, some people say the "Fatima Prayer." In group settings that use it, I've seen everybody say it in unison:

O my Jesus, forgive us our sins, save us from the fires of hell. Lead all souls to heaven, especially those who are in most need of Thy mercy. Amen.

This prayer is completely optional, and not everybody uses it. It's not part of my own practice, but it's popular enough that I'd be remiss in not including it here.

Now that you've completed the first Mystery, you move on to the second one. This begins at the next solitary bead, where you announce the Mystery and say the Our Father, then say ten Hail Mary's, followed by the Glory Be to the Father. Repeat this process until you've completed all five of the day's Mysteries.

6. At the Medal. The Hail, Holy Queen.
Once you've finished the final Mystery, you'll find yourself back at the medal. On this medal you'll say the "Hail, Holy Queen." In group settings, everybody says it in unison:

Hail, Holy Queen, Mother of Mercy, our life, our sweetness, and our hope. To thee to we cry, poor banished children of Eve. To thee do we send up our sighs, mourning and weeping in this valley of tears. Turn then, most gracious advocate, thine eyes of mercy toward us, and after this exile, show unto us the blessed Fruit of thy womb, Jesus. O clement, O loving, O sweet Virgin Mary.

Followed by this versicle and response. In group settings, the leader says the "V" part and the group says the "R" part. In private devotion you say the whole thing yourself:

V. Pray for us, O Queen of the Most Holy Rosary.
R. That we may be made worthy of the promises of Christ.

Afterward you finish say this prayer. In group settings the leader says the prayer while the group says "Amen."

Let us pray,
O God, whose only begotten Son, by His life, death, and resurrection, has purchased for us the rewards of eternal salvation. Grant, we beseech Thee, that while meditating on these mysteries of the most holy Rosary of the Blessed Virgin Mary, that we may both imitate what they contain and obtain what they promise, through Christ our Lord. Amen.

One this last prayer is completed, you close the day's Rosary by making the Sign of the Cross.

6a. What to Do if You're Protestant

Okay, if you're Protestant, you may be thinking "Wow. I can't do this. There is **absolutely no way** I can say that *Hail Holy Queen* prayer!" Well, you're only half right.

You're half right because in group settings the most commonly used prayer is the "Hail Holy Queen." The good news is that there are other prayers that can be substituted; an example is the Lutheran Rosary which substitutes the *Lutheran Hail Mary*, the

Magnificat (Luke 1:46-55), or Martin Luther's *"Evangelical Praise to the Mother of God."*

Lutheran Hail Mary:
Hail Mary, full of grace. The Lord is with thee; blessed art thou among women and blessed is the fruit of thy womb, Jesus Christ. Amen!

Magnificat (text from the *Lutheran Service Book*):
My soul magnifies the Lord, *
and my spirit rejoices in God, my Savior;

For He has regarded *
the lowliness of His handmaiden.

For behold, from this day *
all generations will call me blessed.

For the Mighty One has done great things to me, *
and holy is His name;

And His mercy is on those who fear Him *
from generation to generation.

He has shown strength with his arm; *
He has scattered the proud in the imagination of their hearts.

He has cast down the mighty from their thrones *
and has exalted the lowly.

He has filled the hungry with good things, *
and the rich He has sent empty away.

He has helped his servant Israel in remembrance of his mercy *

as He spoke to our fathers, to Abraham and to his seed forever.

Glory be to the Father, and to the Son, and to the Holy Spirit. *
As I was in the beginning, is now, and ever shall be, world without end. Amen.

Evangelical Praise to the Mother of God:
O Blessed Virgin, Mother of God, what great comfort God has shown us in you, by so graciously regarding your unworthiness and low estate. This encourages us to believe that henceforth He will not despise us poor and lowly ones, but graciously regard us also, according to your example.

After choosing one of these prayers, you may either close the Rosary with the Sign of the Cross, or omit the versicle and say the "*O God, Whose only-begotten Son*" prayer from above before closing with the Sign of the Cross.

7. We're Done

This concludes our tour of the basic method for praying the Rosary, along with some things to expect in a group setting and possible alternate prayers. In the next chapter we'll begin an exploration of the Mysteries themselves before moving on to more advanced methods for turning your Rosary into an Ultimate Weapon for Prayer.

3. The Joyful Mysteries

The Rosary is the Christian's Tree of Life, its 15 traditional Mysteries a garden of roses rather than pomegranates, a treasure-trove of diamonds rather than sapphires. Its meditations are pathworkings not only into the Life of Christ and the development of each Mystery's virtue, but it is through the eyes of Mary that we see the evolutionary progression of our very souls.

At the beginning of the Rosary's cycle we find the *Joyful* or *Joyous Mysteries*. These Mysteries are analogous to the *Illuminative State* of the spiritual life, in which "the mind becomes more enlightened as to spiritual things and the practice of virtue."

In fact the Rosary's Mysteries are themselves an analogy for spiritual development, best understood when we put ourselves in the place of Mary's own journey as she either watches or participates in these scenes in the life, death, and resurrection of her Son. If both Catholics and the original Protestants held up Mary as an example for us to follow, then it's by putting ourselves in her vantage point that we can see how she *became* that example, and then use that example to grow and mature as we walk our own respective paths.

1. The Annunciation

The Annunciation is the first Mystery of the entire Rosary, the beginning of Jesus' entry into the world at the moment the Archangel Gabriel announced this news to Mary. Several things are important as we study this Mystery, as by sending Gabriel to ask her consent, the Biblical text makes it clear God respected Mary's free will.

Another thing of note is the spiritual fruit of this Mystery: *humility*. At the start of our spiritual journey, our two biggest enemies are inertia and pride. Inertia in the sense of laziness or the lack of discipline to persevere on our spiritual path (elsewhere I've called this *hysteresis*), pride that keeps us from seeing our sins and/or counterproductive habits, and pride in the sense of thinking we're perfectly okay the way we are, or don't need to listen to others' advice or correction. Mary did *not* shy away from Gabriel's words, and although she had the option, Mary was humble not to say "No" to God.

While some "traditions" claim discernment is the beginning of the spiritual journey, it's actually humility where this journey begins. Psychologists have long known of the "Dunning-Kruger Effect," for example, where people with no knowledge in a subject parade around like they're experts. This effect is an example of pride getting in the way of discernment, since they're too proud to listen to others and discern how much they don't know. If "pride goeth before the fall," then indeed humility goeth before the rise.

When we realize that the Annunciation is the beginning both of Mary's journey with Jesus and of Jesus' journey upon this physical plane, we can realize that meditating on this Mystery can help us not only learn the virtue of humility and discern or strengths as well as our shortcomings, it can also help us find ways toward new beginnings and speeding our intentions into manifestation.

2. The Visitation

When we move to the second Mystery of the Rosary, we follow Mary, three months pregnant, as she walks across the desert sands to assist her cousin Elizabeth. The spiritual fruit of this Mystery is *charity* or *spiritual love*, and an effect of this love is insight into the various webs of relationships that exist – I call this "the relationship matrix" – between humans, animals, plants, spirits, angels, and maybe even planets and galaxies. This love is not a sanitized or sappy love, but a genuine caring for the well-being of others and a grasp of how the world works such as to understand (and to act) in ways that manifest that charity into real action.

Once we start to see the interrelationships between all things living and their interaction, we can come into what some call a "Vision of the Machinery of the Universe," an epiphany I once described as "seeing the gear-wheels of Heaven," as these webs of relationships start to make sense and we start realizing our place in this vast sea of infinity.

When we meditate on this Mystery, not only can it bring us into closer contact with the virtue of charity, it can help us manifest prayers involving love, family, relationships (business as well as romantic or social); likewise this meditation can help us become aware of the interconnections of all life in the complex web of social, biological, and spiritual relationships.

3. The Nativity of Jesus

When nine months' time had passed, Mary found herself in Joseph's hometown of Bethlehem because of a mandatory census. While in Bethlehem her pregnancy came to term, and because there was no room at the inn she was forced to give birth amongst the filth, germs, and stench of animals, urine, and feces in a stable. We moderns tend to sanitize and romanticize the incident with our Nativity Scenes, a few more realistic ways to view these conditions are "disgusting," "death trap," "eww," "it's a miracle she and the baby didn't die," or the first-world entitlement of "I'd *never* be reduced to something like that!" Even if a well-maintained livery stable wouldn't have such a smell in general, the smell of the animals doing their business (and the Holy Family was there not before or after, but *during*) would still be off-putting.

What I'm saying is that unless one has an agricultural background, there's just no way the average first-world person can wrap their head around how nasty and humiliating this incident must've been, let alone the risk of dying from something doctors at the time had no idea existed, let alone could cure. It was *that* bad, and understanding how bad, how undesirable, is the key to unlocking this Mystery.

Central to this Mystery is the "rags to riches" trope that's inspired people of all ages and all times, except in this case it begins as "riches to rags." Here we have the King of Everything allowing himself to be born into the worst and most disgusting situation imaginable, yet his mission was so important that he maintained the detachment necessary to carry it through. From this low point we see his life gradually showing his glory, building up to a crescendo in the drama of his Death and Resurrection, born into a broken world and making it whole: "Behold, I make all things new."

The spiritual fruit of this Mystery is *detachment*, as in having a healthy amount of emotional detachment to see a plan through to its completion, as the Nativity is the completion of the pregnancy begun in the Annunciation. The Nativity is also the point at which the baby Jesus' physical body first manifested outside the womb and into the world.

Meditation on this Mystery can be instrumental both in gaining this detachment without falling into derangement, in learning to focus one's mind without becoming distracted, and in hastening the physical manifestation of whatever's needed (money, food, etc.) to sustain your current physical condition. Likewise through this detachment we can come to see what needs to be done in getting out of unfavorable situations and working ourselves into a position where we have more control over our lives.

4. The Presentation in the Temple

Forty days after Jesus' birth, we move from the filth of the manger to a much cleaner place, the Temple in Jerusalem. Here Mary fulfils her obligation to the Jewish Law, to be purified after giving childbirth (see Leviticus 12). The Temple this day is a scene for great things, as Simeon, the just man of Jerusalem, begins singing the *Nunc Dimittis* upon recognizing Jesus as the Savior, and the prophetess Anna likewise prophesied of Jesus' importance in the work of redemption.

On the surface, the spiritual fruit of this Mystery is *obedience to divine law*. Yet this makes it real easy to think we're only talking about divine law as written in the Bible and/or any relevant pronouncements by the Church. We have to bear in mind that divine law also includes the laws governing nature, because God made those laws too: gravity, inertia, photosynthesis, even the laws of human nature.

I'm not the first to bring up this point. Francis Collins, former director of the Human Genome Project and director of the National Institute of Health as of this writing, once stated in 2006:

"*The God of the Bible is also the God of the genome. He can be worshipped in the cathedral or in the laboratory. His creation is majestic, awesome, intricate, and beautiful.*"

Nearly 400 years prior, the English philosopher Francis Bacon wrote on a similar vein about the laws of science and nature, and that man can only increase his dominion by recognizing and obeying those laws:

"*Now the empire of man over things depends wholly on the arts and sciences. For we cannot command nature except by obeying her.*"

In, fact traditional (pre-1960) theology textbooks have a term for man's ability to figure out nature's laws: *natural revelation*. The following comes from

Charles Coppens' *Systematic Study of the Catholic Religion*, dated 1903:

"**Revelation** *is the removal of a veil. When the discovery of truth is made by our natural powers, it is called* **natural revelation**."
(Emphasis in original)

All this means that when we meditate upon this Mystery, we're looking to pull water from a well that runs very deep. We can appeal to this Mystery to develop within ourselves the virtue of obedience to divine law, and likewise to help with our learning and application of the natural and social sciences, engineering, mechanical work, and so forth. By extension this Mystery can help us in matters of human law, authority relationships, and matters involving ethical or moral decisions.

Ultimately, by coming to perceive the extensiveness of God's Law and the vastness of the Universe it governs, we can only be brought further into what some call the "Vision of Glory."

5. The Finding in the Temple

We've fast-forwarded twelve years, and again find ourselves with Mary and Joseph in Jerusalem. After they left – was presumably by caravan, as it was a pilgrimage and there's safety in numbers – it took three days to realize they'd left Jesus behind in Jerusalem. Can we imagine the fear in a mother's heart upon realizing her child was lost?

They went back to Jerusalem, their fears relieved upon finding Jesus safe and sound in the Temple, then astonished to find him confounding the Doctors and Scholars of the Jewish Law. When asked about this, the pre-teen Jesus simply stated that he "must be about my Father's business." Mary didn't understand, but she kept the word in her heart while her Son "grew in favor with God and man."

As we unpack this Mystery, we can find that the Joyful Mysteries are marked by emotional lows leading to spiritual highs.

The danger and shame of a 15-year old girl to consent to pregnancy (by someone not her husband) for the sake of helping bring God the Son into the world.

The discomfort of walking the desert leading up to the joyful strains of the *Magnificat*.

The degradation of the stable leading to the angels singing *Gloria in Excelsis Deo*.

The depression of a mother being told her child will be slandered and "a sword will pierce her heart," paired with the high of knowing that child's great role in then-future history.

The fear and anxiety of losing your son, leading to the high of seeing him outsmart the greatest scholars in the big city.

This pattern teaches us a lesson, namely the lesson that in the early stages of our own spirituality, it's through giving up parts of our old selves that we begin to see through to new life (as Christ himself is New Life in full). Putting on that New Life isn't an easy process, and in fact there are times when we'll be downright miserable. If anything, the Joyful Mysteries are a lesson in finding God in the midst of our heartache and suffering, and an indication that as we progress in this New Life, our suffering will eventually come to an end and give way to New Joy.

The talk about joy, as I mean it, isn't some superficial or "warm and fuzzy" clap-trap, because I believe that method's just a way to keep people "minding their place" while telling them "they should be happy for what they have" in exchange for a piein-the-sky future life. No, this book is aimed not so much at an afterlife, so much as it's intended for *helping you in this life right now*. And if I've learned anything in traversing through this life, it's that the greatest cause of misery – in our modern first-world society – is ignorance. It's when we're ignorant of our options and ignorant of how to discern our options, that we wallow in this or that form of misery without hope for improving our condition.

All of this can be detected in the final Joyful Mystery, whose spiritual fruit is *turning* or *conversion to Christ-ward*, and is integral to what I just said about suffering leading to joy and a "Vision of Beauty." When we meditate on this Mystery, we can appeal to it for conversion of ourselves to a deeper following of Christ and likewise that of our loved ones. On a deeper level we can appeal to this Mystery for a breaking away of ignorance in ourselves and others, for opening our eyes to realize our proverbial "blind spots" and realize our options for self-improvement, for overcoming and/or healing our weaknesses (physical, mental, emotional), and for helping others come around to see out point of view – not necessarily convince them, but at least help them to see and understand where we're coming from.

4. The Sorrowful Mysteries

While the Joyful Mysteries center on Mary's life as she gives both to Jesus and watches over his childhood, the Sorrowful Mysteries focus entirely on the person of Jesus over roughly an 18-hour period from the Last Supper to the Crucifixion. These Mysteries are bloody, violent, and would be considered downright inappropriate for children to witness had they taken place in modern times. These Mysteries are related to the *Purgative State* of the spiritual life, which is concerned with overcoming vices in order that the soul may become a field of virtues.

6. The Agony in the Garden

After the Last Supper, Jesus and the Apostles went to the garden in Gethsemane, where he prayed over the coming day's events: "*Let this cup pass from me.*" He knew what was going to happen, and I don't think any of us can blame him for having second thoughts about it.

Yet in the end, Jesus resigned himself to the kangaroo court, mockery, torture, and death that was to come: "*Not my will, but thine be done.*"

This Mystery, like most of the Sorrowful Mysteries, is fairly straightforward in its message. Its spiritual fruit is *submission to divine will*, which in turn makes it a corollary of the Fourth Joyful Mystery: the Presentation embodies the virtue to obey divine law, while the Agony seeks to overcome our internal obstacles that keep us from that obedience. Meditation and appeal to this Mystery can assist us in discovering and overcoming our own problems, confront deep-seated issues keeping you from reaching your full potential, giving us the courage to start a new task, overcome competition or lawsuits when our cause is just, help us to overcome trust issues in ourselves and others, and find the courage and energy (through trust in God) to realize our full potential.

7. The Scourging at the Pillar

The next scene begins after Jesus was brought to court on false charges and convicted by the testimony of false witnesses. The Sanhedrin took him before Pilate to pass judgment, and Pilate ordered him scourged.

The Romans were particularly good at torture, and their scourges were often made of cords with glass or bone shards knotted into them. These were designed to rip skin off the victim's body – think of the potential for infection or worse in these conditions – and it was common for the recipient to die.

The spiritual fruit of this Mystery is *control over our physical urges*, which can run the gamut from hypersexuality to overeating. The concern here isn't with suppression (which leads to psychological problems later on), but with getting these urges under your conscious control.

Meditation and appeal to this Mystery can assist with gaining that control, and in can help in relationship issues by getting an unreciprocated admirer to back off. As a control over urges, this Mystery can be helpful in ending relationships that have gone on "past their expiration date," and this Mystery's association with brutality makes it helpful for finding one's way out of an abusive situation.

8. The Crowning with Thorns

As we contemplate these Mysteries, it's easy to compartmentalize them as separate events, but we have to remember that in real-time everything came at Jesus fast. One of the first rules of torture is not to give the victim a pause to collect his thoughts or build up any kind of mental resolve, so everything that happened, happened in rapid succession.

After Jesus was brutalized – skin peeled off his body, agonizing in excruciating pain, and possibly in hypovolemic shock from the loss of blood – the soldiers wrapped him in a purple robe and placed a crown of thorns upon his head, then mocked him by shouting "*Ave, Rex Judaeórum!*" The false trial, the scourging, and now this; if the Joyful Mysteries were marked by highs and lows, the Sorrowful Mysteries can best be described as one massive low getting progressively lower.

In Jesus' humiliation, we're shown the face of our own pride, and the spiritual fruit of this Mystery is *control over our thoughts and emotions*. If the Annunciation bears the fruit of humility, then the Crowning with Thorns brings the wherewithal to tear down whatever barrier stands in the way of reaching that humility. In learning control over our thoughts and emotions, we learn to subdue pride as well as anything else blocking that "still, small voice" of God speaking to us.

This Mystery, in short, helps us to get control over our own minds. As an uncontrolled mind is one that misses opportunities, so meditating or appealing to this Mystery can also help you organize your life and maximize the opportunities for success, and can also be used on behalf of others seeking to get a handle on themselves.

Appeal to this Mystery likewise can help one toward finding peace within oneself (by confronting buried emotional baggage or other obstacles in the way if necessary), and for helping to establish peace within a community. The reason is that when people can get a better handle on their emotions, it's easier to work past their differences and work past objects of contention insofar as such cooperation is possible.

9. The Carrying of the Cross

Jesus' torture continues, as now he's forced to carry a heavy wooden cross from the city all the way to the place where he's to be put to death. Beaten, bloodied, thorns on his head, possibly in shock, and his clothes likely sticking to his body thanks to all the bleeding and possibly peeled-off skin, Jesus takes up the cross and soldiers on until he can carry it no more.

If anything can be said about this Mystery, it's that its spiritual fruit is *perseverance*. How many times have we found ourselves not wanting to go on with something we're planning, that it's too much just to get out of bed and go to work anymore? How often have we look at some project to improve our lives, worked at it for a week, then decided it was too much trouble and just gave up on it?

That's where meditation and appeal to this Mystery come in: perseverance, the strength and willpower to keep at something, patience, the will to see a project through to completion, and to some degree empowerment in the ability to persevere. This Mystery can be useful especially to spiritual novices and entrepreneurs, and others whose goals involve sticking it out through long-range planning.

10. The Crucifixion

You've probably figured out something about me: I like my Nativity Scenes poopy and my Crucifixes bloody. That's because I don't like my religion sanitized; I like my religion in-your-face and *real*. And as we approach Jesus' last moments, we find his life every bit as messy and chaotic as the night he was delivered in the manger.

If the Sorrowful Mysteries are a series of pains and humiliations dog-piled one on top of the other, then the final act is a real curtain closer. Broken, bloodied, bruised, derided, in shock, his clothes sticking to his body, forced to carry a heavy piece of wood, and exhausted beyond what many of us can imagine – the soldiers now rip Jesus' clothes off his body and we can only imagine the pain as it's torn from his exposed wounds.

As Jesus is then nailed to the cross, imagine what blood is left pouring out through his hands and feet. For three hours he hung upon the cross, fluids gathering in his chest. Yet even in this state of disgrace and utter despair, he said words of forgiveness upon his persecutors and all who mocked him; finally, he gave up the ghost and died.

In the epilogue to *The Magic of Catholicism*, I wrote that this Mystery is a climax, the intent being that this is a "jumping-off point" for the soul:

In the Fifth Sorrowful Mystery, we now witness the climax to all the Mysteries which have come before it, and the gateway to all those which will come after it. For here the soul has learned its lessons and persevered in the work of perfection, but in its submission to God and pursuit of the spirit, at some point the soul must die to the world. It must die to the world so that it may transcend the world. It must die to the world so that it may forgive the offenses, real or perceived, which have been heaped upon it by the world. As the soul has gained virtues and had the corresponding vices purged, so must the soul eventually die to those vices, that it may transcend them. . . . Having become purged of those vices, of pride, of avarice, of lust, and of disobedience, we die to them, that we may emerge from the tomb in glory.

It is this point, where in the Crucifixion, the soul's darkest night, we actually find ourselves with one foot in two worlds. We live in a world where self-appointed "gurus" try selling us a "no fuss, no muss" spirituality, or sermons tell us you can have your "prosperity" cake and eat it too. But the ancient wisdom of Christianity thunders through both East and West, and we have analogues of it in other religions with long histories as well: there is no gain without sacrifice; there is no new growth without clearing away old structures; there is no power in spirituality that rejects renunciation.

As you read this, I don't want you to think I'm glorifying in suffering for the sake of suffering, because nothing could be further from the truth. In several other places I've railed against the "offer it up" mentality that encourages Catholics to mind their place and bear their pains without hope of ever overcoming them. To put it simply, **suffering and renunciation are only good when you grow, improve, and gain from the process. Suffering and renunciation are USELESS when you merely wallow in it, ignore it, or merely accept it as "your lot in life."**

The Crucifixion is unique amongst the Mysteries in that it contains two spiritual fruits: *dying to self* and *forgiveness of others' trespasses*. Both these fruits, valuable as they are, are like leaves on the stem of a much hardier fruit: *completely letting your old self go*.

Completely letting your old self go, becoming free of old habits and thought-processes, emptying oneself of sour milk and stagnant water so as to be filled with fresh and new drink – these are the results of this Mystery's spiritual fruits, and meditating upon this Mystery can help toward bring an end to bad or long-expired circumstances in your life, manifesting forgiveness as proper and necessary, and emptying out the old to make way for the new.

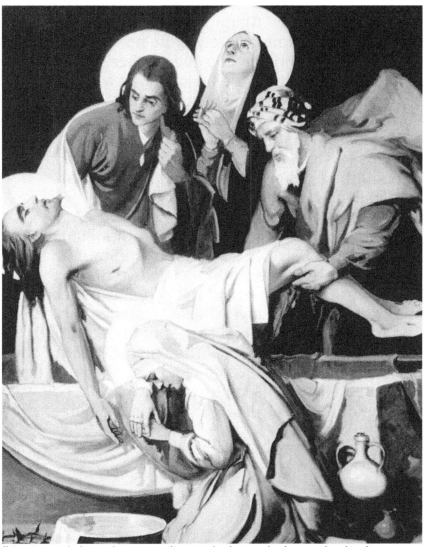

"So Joseph bought some linen cloth, took down the body, wrapped it in the linen, and placed it in a tomb cut out of rock. Then he rolled a stone against the entrance of the tomb. Mary Magdalene and Mary the mother of Joseph saw where he was laid."

– Mark 15:46-47 (NIV)

5. The Glorious Mysteries

If the Sorrowful Mysteries move from one low to an even lower one, the Glorious Mysteries pick up where that low left off, immediately bringing us to a great "high" and then bringing us ever higher still. If the Joyful Mysteries show the beginning of a process coupled with glimpses of what *could* be, the Sorrowful Mysteries tear down the obstacles in man and prepare him for becoming. As we move to the Glorious Mysteries, we see what man can become as through the eyes of one who has *become* that potential.

While the Joyful Mysteries represent the Illuminative State and the Sorrowful the Purgative State, the Glorious Mysteries relate to the *Unitive State*, the union with God by love and the actual experience and exercise of that love. These Mysteries can be said to represent the final stages of the soul's journey on what some call "The Path of Return," the stages in which the devotee is now purified and now walks in union with God here on Earth while being assured of sitting at His right hand in the hereafter.

11. The Resurrection

For two days Jesus' body has lain in the tomb, Friday being the first day and Saturday being the second. Because Saturday was the "shabbos," or the legally-mandated day of rest, it was on the third day, Sunday, that a group of women went to the tomb to anoint Jesus' body. When they got there, the tomb was empty, and the resurrected Jesus began showing himself to the women, the Apostles, and the disciples.

When we meditate on this Mystery, it helps to begin by realizing we're in the place of the women who first saw the tomb. The body of Jesus was now the corpse of a known criminal, specifically a blasphemer, and this means his followers could likewise be charged and executed for blasphemy. In other words, we're talking about some very scared people here, yet these women worked up the courage to go out to the tomb (tacitly identify themselves as followers of Jesus) and care for the body buried there.

Cliff Notes version: we have to begin by contemplating *fear*.

Yet when they got to the tomb, the Synoptic Gospels (Matthew, Mark, and Luke) all tell us an angel (or two) appeared at the tomb and announced to them that Jesus had risen from the dead. Each Gospel differs on the precise details, though the broad strokes are the same.

These women went from being *afraid* to being *filled with joy*.

And this is the key to the First Glorious Mystery, that mental movement from overwhelming fear to overwhelming joy. If the Crucifixion is the "dark night of the soul," then the Resurrection is our "rosy dawn" in which we've traversed the abyss and find ourselves with sure footing on the other side of the chasm.

This ties into the spiritual fruit of the Resurrection, namely *firmness of faith*. The Gospels and Acts of the Apostles tell us that Jesus appeared both to the women and to the rest of the believers after his resurrection, proving he actually came back from the dead and teaching them over a period of forty days (Acts 1:3). Later, Paul tells us that Jesus appeared to no less than 500 people (1 Corinthians 15:6), and that "if Christ has not been raised, our preaching is useless and so is your faith" (15:14/NIV).

How is our faith so intrinsically tied to the Resurrection? We have to remember that any person can die; dying doesn't necessarily prove anything special. But when's the last time you saw an average Joe come back from the dead? And I don't mean near-death experiences or narcolepsy (the ancients knew about these things too), I mean verified dead and after well over 48 hours had passed.

This, in a nutshell, is why the Resurrection is tied to firmness of faith, because it is the *proof* of our faith. The Apostles were so confident that it happened, that Christianity admits having no reason to exist if it Jesus didn't come back from the dead. And it's in this transition from grief and fear to joy and celebration, this proof of every last article of faith that we encounter as we pray this Mystery.

When we pray this Mystery with the intent of bringing results into our life, we find this Mystery lends itself well toward learning to defend one's faith and protecting loved ones from being evangelized by people who want them to abandon their own beliefs. This Mystery also lends itself to helping with gaining constancy of will and works of renewal after a massive loss or a bad downturn, whether this renewal is needed in the sphere of love, business, health, or any other area of life.

12. The Ascension

The Book of Acts can also be called "The Gospel of Luke, Part II," and in fact scholars often refer to "Luke-Acts" as a way of pointing out the two books' continuity. It begins like a sort of follow-up letter to a recipient named "Theophilus" (the name literally means "Lover of God"), and immediately goes into telling the rest of the story:

1. Jesus remained on earth 40 days after his resurrection.
2. Jesus taught during those 40 days.
3. After that time Jesus ascended into heaven.

What we see in this Mystery is the continuation of a process. The Joyful Mysteries are about *Preparation*, the Sorrowful Mysteries are about *Struggle and Purgation*, while the Glorious Mysteries are a process of *Completion*. In the Ascension, we're seeing two parts of the process completed.

First, we have to consider that the spiritual fruit of the Ascension is *Longing to be in Heaven*. This is a completion of the indifference to the physical universe that's the fruit of the Third Joyful Mystery, which we see reflected through overcoming our base passions in the Second Sorrowful. Here in the Second Glorious Mystery we find ourselves having come out the other side of those processes and our eyes fixed solely on Heaven as our true home. By extension, longing for a place means utilizing all the virtues we've learned along the way in terms doing what we need to get there.

This one process we see completed. Another process we find here is the process of the Glorious Mysteries themselves. This process begins with the Resurrection, in which the soul has conquered its vices and unshackled itself from the subconscious chains mooring it to the physical and/or to an inclination toward sin. In the Ascension, this process continues with the soul no longer looking back but forward to its new life and its new home.

To pray this Mystery is to bring into one's life an abundance of clarity and hope, namely because where the Nativity brings us a big-picture view of the situation, the Ascension manifests a deeper level of that big-picture view. Such a penetrating view can only bring hope because we're seeing things as they exist in the context of God's providence. This can help with long-range planning and with "ironing out the bugs" that pop up sooner or later in any strategy. This Mystery also teaches us that if we wish to enter our spiritual home, we must first conquer and transcend the temptations, influences, and limitations of this one; we can learn exactly how to do this by working through the Nativity, the Scourging, and the Ascension in that order.

13. The Descent of the Holy Ghost

When it comes to details, Luke-Acts does not fail to deliver. Immediately after Jesus departs for heaven, Luke tells us what Peter, Mary, the rest of the Apostles, and the disciples (followers who weren't Apostles) did for the next nine days.

We're told these believers, numbering one hundred and twenty, spent their days in prayer in an "upper room" in Jerusalem; this is considered the origin of the *Novena*, or nine days' prayer. We're also told the Apostles chose Matthias to replace Judas after he'd betrayed Jesus and hung himself. This is the Biblical basis for *Apostolic Succession*, the doctrine that the apostles chose a successor to Judas, and in time these successors chose their successors; these successors are the bishops of the Catholic and Orthodox Churches.

Finally, on the tenth day, Luke tells us the Holy Ghost came down from heaven and tongues of fire descended on everyone in the entire house, who then began speaking in other languages as the Spirit enabled them. (Acts 2:2-4)

The rest of Acts tells the story of the early Christian community, focusing on Paul's journeys, the development of Christianity's shift away from Judaism, and most importantly the power of the Holy Ghost that infused the Apostle's mission, work, and preaching.

The Descent of the Holy Ghost is a higher analogue to two of the Joyous Mysteries, in that it finishes the process begun in the Finding in the Temple, and renews the process begun in the Annunciation. It completes the first, because the spiritual fruit of this Mystery – being infused with the gifts of the Holy Ghost – is the result of consistently converting one's life to Christ, who promised to send the Spirit to his disciples (John 16:7). This also renews the process begun in the Annunciation, because it we are now being infused with the Spirit that infused Mary; just as she bore fruit, so are we expected to go forth and bear fruits according to what we've been given.

Likewise this Mystery is a completion of the Crowning with Thorns, as it is through the conquering of one's stray thoughts and emotions that we begin to discern the Holy Ghost filling us and working through us. We have to remember that the Holy Ghost moves and penetrates through all creation (theologians call this *perichoresis*), but it's only when we've learned self-discipline that we can become effective "at-will" channels for the Holy Ghost's grace and power. Thus the progression here is that we convert our lives to Christ-ward and win the battle over our emotional passions, after which we become effective channels of grace in the world as we currently inhabit it.

While appeal to this Mystery can be used to bring about a heavy influx of Divine Power as well as love, understanding, and self-transformation (i.e. the seven gifts of the Holy Ghost, described in Isaiah 11:2-3), this Mystery is also a higher analogue of The Visitation in that its implications are *social* as well as *individual*. That is, the disciples didn't receive the Holy Ghost just so they could stay in the Upper Room and keep praying, they received the Holy Ghost so they could go out into the world and *do something that matters*. As a lamp isn't hidden under a bowl, this means the Holy Ghost is given to you so you can share with others.

Now I'll immediately state what when I talk about making a difference, I don't mean "social justice" or political activism. These things are valid paths when done in accordance with traditional Christian teaching, but they are not the only paths. Another path can consist of building something for yourself with what you've learned, then going forth and helping teach others how to do the same; this is the "teach a man how to fish" model, which I prefer over "give a man a fish" because it helps them acquire the skills to become independent and enables them to pass it on. This way you're effectively lighting another candle from the flame inside you, which in turn can light other candles, and so on.

There are other paths to reach out into the world and exercise that charity which is a gift of the Holy Ghost, and some may take longer to implement than others, some may require more resources than others, and various other factors. So don't rush in and say "I'm gonna do this!" Instead, give yourself time to prayer and meditation, and listen to that still, small voice to tell you when the time is to go out into the world and what's the best way to go about doing it.

14. The Assumption of Mary

With the Assumption of Mary, we move outside the Biblical narrative and into the stories of Church tradition. We also move into the private life of Mary, a privacy she no longer had once her Son had gone public with his own ministry.

Tradition has it that she moved to Ephesus and lived another fifteen years after Jesus' ascension. When the day came, the Apostles attended her funeral except Thomas who seems to have a habit of being late for important occasions. When Thomas finally made it there, he and the Apostles went to see her grave and hound it empty except for the smell of lilies.

Now, we have no idea whether this story is true and no way of substantiating it. But we do know what the Church teaches, that at the moment of her death, Jesus rewarded his Mother by bringing ("assuming") her body and soul into heaven.

If you're a Traditional Roman Catholic, then you already believe this without question. If you're a Novus Ordinarian (a "post-Vatican II" Catholic), then you may either believe it wholeheartedly or just say the words but not necessarily believe it in your chest. If you're a Protestant, then you'll just as likely say "Hogwash!" and close the book, or keep reading so you'll find something to laugh at. Personally, I don't care whether you believe in the Assumption as a literal and historical fact; my point isn't to debate historical narratives but to discuss operative principles.

The main principle here can be discerned in light of this Mystery's spiritual fruit, which is "the grace of a happy death." What we see in this is an allusion to completion, to the reward for a job well done. To borrow an analogy, we could (very sloppily) make a comparison to the Buddhist concept of *Nirvana* or "snuffing out," the phase where the work of "ending desire" is complete and before *Moksha* or "final liberation."

This is a sloppy comparison because it's apples-to-oranges, but the general principle of "completion before final reward" is very much in play here.

A happy death and a finished work can be associated with a peaceful rest, this Mystery can be seen as a higher analogue to the Carrying of the Cross in that appeal to it can go a long way toward seeing a work towards its completion. This Mystery's association with death can also assist in works geared toward nurturing or applying indulgences to the Poor Souls in purgatory in general and deceased loved ones in particular.

15. The Coronation of Mary

In addition to Mary's assumption, Traditional Catholics believe that Mary was given a crown of twelve stars after Jesus brought her into heaven, and the title "Queen of Heaven." Other titles such as "Empress of the Universe" and "Co-Redemptrix and Mediatrix of All Graces" also abound.

While all the other Mysteries are about process, and some are higher analogues of others, the Mystery of the Coronation is about *fulfillment* and *completion*. The Coronation crowns all the other Mysteries, is a higher analogue to all the Mysteries, and completes their entire cycle. In this Mystery we see the soul having conquered, having completed its quest, and now having seen its reward. While the Assumption brings us the final liberation from the chains of matter and the struggle against the powers of darkness, it's in the Coronation that the soul ultimately receives its just reward and – as Mary was crowned and then looked back with favor on the human race – for the soul to look back upon those who need its help as well.

The spiritual fruit of this Mystery is *receiving the crown that awaits us in heaven,* and this can be expanded to mean *receiving a just reward according to one's life.* This "crown that awaits us" is the crown given to the Saints who've gone before us, and who now look upon us and intercede in our times of need. In this case we see that while the Descent of the Holy Ghost implies a vertical relationship with God and a horizontal relationship with our fellow-men, in the Coronation the soul enters into a vertical relationship with its former fellow-men and a horizontal with its fellow-saints, who are all empowered by a vertical relationship with God.

Appeal to this Mystery can assist in works of manifesting justice, revealing those falsely accused and guilty parties who've been overlooked. This Mystery can also be helpful in works attempting to establish unity towards completing a purpose (as the Coronation unifies all the other Mysteries by being their goal), and this can be applied on the spiritual level as well as on the physical. Likewise, this Mystery can also be appealed in conjunction with the others to lend extra blessing to the work at hand.

6. Pathworking the Mysteries

In the last few chapters, I mentioned "appeal to this Mystery can bring such and such a result." However, we don't pray the Rosary by focusing on one Mystery all the way through. We instead pray the entire set of Mysteries as we go.

So how do we appeal to each Mystery in particular as an overarching theme for our Rosary? The way we do this is something called a *Pathworking*.

In former times, the term "pathworking" had a very specific meaning, but has come to refer to any sort of guided meditation and visualization session.

Can a Christian Do This?

While pathworking is a product of not-exactly Christian schools of thought, it is permitted for a Christian to use it, under the following conditions:

"Just as 'the Catholic Church rejects nothing of what is true and holy in these religions,' neither should [non-Christian] ways be rejected out of hand simply because they are not Christian. On the contrary, one can take from them what is useful so long as the Christian conception of prayer, its logic and requirements are never obscured."
    – Ratzinger, *Letter to the Bishops on Some Aspects of Christian Meditation*, 1989

In this case, we take the general method of pathworking and place it within a Christian theological matrix, thus fulfilling the requirements stated above.

Visualization Training

The method of pathworking is simple, though it may take some getting used to if you don't have trouble seeing images in your mind. If that's the case, then take a few minutes each day trying to picture simple shapes: squares, circles, triangles; there's nothing special here, just try to hold these images in your mind. For some people it's easier to do with their eyes closed and for others with eyes open; find which way works best for you and stick with it.

Do this whenever you find a few spare minutes at work, or between classes, when waking up in the morning, after supper in the evening, whenever you can find the time. Once you succeed at holding an image in your mind for a couple minutes, then try imagining it in different colors, or you can imagine it spinning or otherwise moving around.

After you're proficient with shapes, you can move on to three dimensional objects, like an apple, and imagine the look of the apple, the feel of the apple when you touch it, the smell when you cut into it, the sound when you bite into it, and the taste when you eat it.

Once you've mastered this step, at this point you're exercising all five senses in your visualizations and seeing in three dimensions. **You're ready to begin pathworking**.

Method for Pathworking

All you need for a pathworking is a chair and a dark room. Sit down, breathe deeply, and relax. Feel all the tension leaving you and let your mind go blank.

If you visualize better with your eyes closed, then close them. If not, then leave them open.

In your mind, create a stylized image of the Mystery you wish to contemplate. This image could be a Roman numeral between I and XV, or it can be a symbol associated with what's going on in the Mystery (a manger, a crown of thorns, etc.). Visualize it in front of you.

Step through this styled image as though you were walking through a door. It could function like a hinged door, a curtain, or a sliding door like in the supermarket or a science-fiction film. Whatever seems more natural to you.

On the other side of the "door," you walk into the scene of the Mystery. Take a moment to observe it, listen for any sounds, overhear any conversations from bystanders and so forth. Also notice the location of Jesus and Mary.

Once you've observed, go and have an imaginary conversation with people in the scene. This is all in your head and may feel silly, but it can help you; what the people say can be considered parts of your subconscious talking to you, and can help you realize whether you actually want whatever it is you're praying for, or if you might have other options to make things happen.

If possible, make your way to Jesus and Mary. Discuss your problem with them alongside any possible solutions and exactly what it is you're praying for. Make the conversation as specific and detailed as possible, and pay attention to any feedback.

After this conversation is over, thank them and make your way back to the portal you used to enter the scene. Walk through it again and imagine the image disappearing. Whenever you're ready, get out of the chair and turn on the lights.

You may feel a little "woozy" after this exercise. If that's the case, then go to the kitchen and grab a glass of water or make yourself a sandwich.

Why Did We Do This?

Now for the fun part, the *why* part. As in, "Why did I just do this crazy exercise that's all in my head?"

Well, you're right, it *is* all in your head, and you just did two very useful things. The first thing you did was link yourself to your subconscious, which gave you a feel for whether you really want to do whatever it is you're doing. This also gives you a chance to dialogue with your inner self and probe for any doubts, any uncertainties, any character issues you might have that need to be worked on first. If you're praying out of anger or jealousy, for example, you're not likely to get the results you're looking for .

. . best to find these out and work on them *before* you pray.

The second thing you did was actual prayer. You see, prayer isn't just moving your lips and saying *Our Father*, that's just a form of prayer called *vocal prayer*. The other form of prayer is called *mental prayer*, where you pray in the recesses of your mind. By focusing yourself so totally inward, your conversation with Jesus and Mary becomes a very pure prayer to them. By associating one or other Mystery with your intention, this gives your subconscious (which works in symbols) an important symbolic cue that it can use to amplify the prayer going out from your mind. What we realize here is that prayer as almost as much psychological and emotional as it is spiritual.

When Should I Do This?
In my experience, pathworking immediately before praying the Rosary doesn't work out too well. It seems best to give it an hour or two in between, or to do the pathworking the evening before you pray the Rosary. Likewise I wouldn't advise doing a pathworking every day, but every two or three days while praying the Rosary every day until your intention is accomplished.

7. Ingredients for Effective Prayer

This book is about weaponizing your Rosary to get results, and a large part of the Rosary is about prayer. So let's talk about making your prayers effective.

The Bible tells us to "pray without ceasing" and that "the prayer of the righteous is worth much." We hear this overmuch in churches, but what rarely gets talked about is *how to pray in order to get concrete results*.

In this the churches do a disservice, because the human mind is drawn to "signs and wonders." No matter how much we try to talk ourselves out of that fact (or mentally evade it), the bottom line is that human nature is human nature. Humans are drawn to signs and wonders, and without those signs and wonders – i.e. actual results manifesting in their lives – it's going to take a lot more for the average person to continue believing in God or caring about their parents' faith.

Without further ado, let's get right into this, shall we?

The Seven Keys

There are seven keys to making your prayers fruitful, and I describe them in *The Magic of Effective Prayer*. In order, they are:

1. Love God
2. Love Yourself
3. Love Your Neighbor
4. Attitude of Gratitude

5. Visualize to Actualize
6. Sphere of Availability
7. Ain't Nothin' to It But to Do It!

Excerpts from these chapters can be found on the on the THAVMA blog at http://bit.ly/2jqkDmP, and I'd like to address some items here.

1. Love God

The greatest act of power is the creation of the universe, and that was caused by God acting out of love because, as some traditions say, "God wished to behold God." This love is why we (namely our souls) are made in the image of God, and why God has a connection with us on every level.

Think about it, have you ever loved someone and not felt a connection with them? Mother, father, sibling, spouse, friend, or even your dog or cat? When love is given and returned, this connection moves in both directions.

That God loves us is beyond question. Certainly, this raises debates over the "why is there evil in the world" question, and my own "short answer" is that evil exists because God chooses not to interfere with human free will. This could give rise to a whole thread of theological speculation and argumentation, though it's outside the scope of this book and therefore a thread I'm not going to entertain.

What thread I will entertain is that God's love for us is a connection between him and us, and that our love for God is the affirmation of a reciprocal connection, forming a bond that's unstoppable.

2. Love Yourself

Here we encounter another disservice from a lot of pulpits, the inclination to tell people "You shouldn't love yourself" or "You're an unworthy sinner in the eyes of God." I'd like to point out that not all pulpits do this, but enough do it that we can't throw a stone without hitting at least one person damaged by such belief systems.

Any teaching of self-hatred, or of obliterating one's own personality in favor of an "ideal personality," such teaching is not only un-Biblical – Proverbs 19:8 tells us "To get wisdom is to love yourself" – it's un-Christian.

If I were to hazard a guess, I'd say the fear of self-love has to do with the Fourth Gospel's emphasis on altruism – "Greater love hath no man than this, that a man lay down his life for his friends" (John 15:13/KJV) – and a false sense that self-love is no different from selfishness and a sense of entitlement.

The truth is that selfishness, pride, entitlement, possessiveness, and so forth are imbalanced emotions and have nothing to do with true self-love. **To love yourself is a reflection of loving God, to know firmly that you are created in the image of God, and to return the love that God has for you.**

In plain English this means that by loving ourselves we love God, because our soul is the mirror-image of God. Love of God is cemented in the heart by love of self, and love of self completes the bond that we acknowledge and actively enter into by love of God.

To love oneself requires the ability to have balanced emotions, an accurate picture of who and what we are, and the ability to accept our imperfections while working to turn them into strengths. We may have many obstacles in the path of getting there – childhood experiences, messages from corporate advertising, and so on – but we can clear the negative programming out of our minds and get there. It's a different road for each person, but it's only a question of *how* and *when*.

3. Love Your Neighbor

By loving God and loving yourself, you're acknowledging and participating in a link of love and of power. In loving your neighbor, you take this to the next level.

If to love yourself is to acknowledge you're created in the image of God, then to love your neighbor is to acknowledge he or she is created in the image of God also. In essence you not only participate in a vertical link with God but also a horizontal link with the rest of humanity and perhaps with all of creation.

Diagram of Perichoresis
or Circumincession

Now this doesn't mean to be loving to the point of tolerating wrongdoing or destruction when your neighbor commits it, quite the opposite. It means that for the sake of your other neighbors, you will do what you can to see the offending neighbor is brought to justice. Loving someone means recognizing their freedom to be who they authentically are, but it doesn't mean upholding any freedom to harm others or do evil.

3b. Love and Power

In the preceding Keys, I focused on the word "love," while using it in tandem with the word "power." This is in line with something I tell my students that you should always ask for both love and power. Not one or the other, but always both.

The reason for this is that one upholds and balances the other. Love without power, for example, becomes filled with compassion for the suffering it sees yet is helpless to do anything about it. Others who are not loving can see love as a sign of weakness and take advantage of it, walk all over it, while love by itself is helpless to stop them. This can result in many an initially-loving person becoming cynical and bitter, losing that love thanks to a lack of power.

Power, on the other hand, can do anything it wants. Yet power without love has no sympathy or compassion; it can crush the just and the unjust alike. Power unchecked by love is a ticket either to a dictatorship or the insane asylum; it easily becomes corrupt, psychotic, and delusional.

This is why I tell my students they should always look to both love and power, no matter how out-of-place or difficult the equation seems to them. Those balanced will want to stay in balance, while those imbalanced have a need to become balanced if they wish to succeed in spiritual work. A person's ease (or lack thereof) with the concept of love and power as a both/and, that can help the individual find out whether they need work in a given area.

4. An Attitude of Gratitude

In December of 2015, my van broke down in a Kroger's parking lot. I'd just replaced the alternator that afternoon, so to say I was angry would be an understatement. It didn't help that I'd just moved back to Dayton after 15 years in Columbus, and the town had drastically changed from anything I remember. That added to the frustration, not knowing who was still in business or who to call.

Not long after this happened, a woman walked by, suggested a towing company, and thrust a wad of cash into my hand. Within half an hour everything was taken care of and the tow truck brought my van home safe and sound. If I had any doubts about whether angels exist, I don't have any doubts now.

She didn't give me any contact information and I've never seen her again (I'd like to return the money and thank her profusely), but to this day I'm still grateful. And that type of gratefulness is important to a successful experience of prayer.

When we show gratitude, we take part in returning God's love back to its source, and that love is renewed and returned even more. In *The Magic of*

Effective Prayer I referred to the story of Jesus and the ten lepers (Luke 17:11-19). This story illustrates the importance of gratitude, as of the ten lepers Jesus healed it was only one who came back to thank him. Jesus' response was:

"Jesus asked, 'Were not all ten cleansed? Where are the other nine? Has no one returned to give praise to God except this foreigner?' Then he said to him, 'Rise and go; your faith has made you well.'" (Luke 17:17-19/NIV)

Note that even though Jesus healed the other nine, it was only to the one who came back to give thanks that Jesus said "Your faith has made you well." Giving thanks is an expression of love and appreciation, which leads to more love and appreciation in return.

I truly believe this is why the happiest people I've met were all *thankful* people at heart, while the most miserable people I've met were all either *ungrateful* or constantly *looking for someone to blame* for their problems. Gratitude helps one to recognize the good in God, in themselves, and in their neighbors around them, and recognizing something is a first step toward manifesting it; this continues a cycle of increasing love and increasing manifestation. Lack of gratitude can (though not necessarily always) lead to seeing only the negative in God, self, and neighbor, and not seeing the positive can lead to blindness to opportunity and therefore not manifesting it. Both of these are vicious cycles.

When you pray, be sure to include some from of thanks from time to time, speaking of your intentions as though they've already happened. This is a show of love and a show of believing your prayer has already been answered. As Jesus himself says:

"Therefore I tell you, whatever you ask for in prayer, believe that you have received it, and it will be yours." (Mark 11:24)

5. Visualize to Actualize

We've talked about mental prayer in the chapter on pathworking, and here I'd like to reiterate that visualization is a form of mental prayer. When you pray for something, visualize that "something" as though it had already happened or is already happening. See it unfold in your mind's eye, feel the emotions swell through you as though it had happened, and any feel/smell/taste as they'd apply to that for which you're praying.

One technique that can be helpful here is to write down exactly what you want before you begin praying for it. Write it down exactly, honestly, and in your own words, and then visualize it based on what you wrote. This will further help you determine if what you really want is what you think you want, and it will also help you form a clearer picture in your mind.

Another technique is something called "Treasure Charts," where you find pictures in magazines, Google images, and anywhere else you can find them. Find the images that represent your payer intentions, cut them out or print them – do NOT use these on an electronic screen as the eyes react differently – and put them up on a poster board you can look at while you pray. The purpose is to help as an aid to visualization while you pray to make these intentions real.

6. The Sphere of Availability

This is something I've *never* heard addressed from any pulpit. In fairness, I've not heard every sermon ever preached at every church in the entire world, but it's never been in any of the sermons I have heard.

What the *Sphere of Availability* means is that you can only manifest (and hold onto) something if it's within the radius of what you're able to use. For example, a person without a high school diploma won't likely be able to manifest a CEO job at a Fortune 500 company, because he or she wouldn't have any idea what to do if they got it.

We also see what happens when people somehow *do* manage to manifest something that's outside their sphere. Lottery winners are an excellent example of this: how many times do we hear news stories about someone winning the "big bucks" only to be broke and eyeballs-deep in debt a year or two later? What happened is that they manifested something outside their sphere without acquiring the knowledge to *use* it effectively, and so the dragon of that manifestation set them on fire.

In this sense, I've come to see the Sphere of Availability both as a sign of God's love and as an opportunity for self-advancement. On the one hand, it shows God's love because it protects us from being burned by that which we aren't equipped to use. On the other hand, it gives us an opportunity to improve and advance the gifts God gave us, because we have it within ourselves to *expand* our Sphere of Availability.

So how do we expand the sphere? First, by considering the sphere is influenced by two factors: *opportunity* and *education*. Opportunity is something we can create, especially here in a first-world country, while education is something we can give ourselves in the age of self-help books and Google.

Do you want more money? Then look to see what opportunities surround you. Get a job (even a menial one) until you can afford a car, then get a car and a better job with a car. At the same time read some reputable blogs and books about economics, entrepreneurship, and investing. What happens here is you're creating and expanding opportunities for cash flow, while at the same time learning how money actually works and to recognize opportunities you can leverage into making even more.

Do you want a romantic partner? If you have no social skills and no social life, that's not going to happen immediately. Instead, expand your opportunities by finding groups of like-minded people and making friends, while at the same time learning reading and working on developing your people skills. One thing will lead to another as your sphere expands.

You may notice that in both these examples, I didn't mention prayer. That was intentional, since I'm assuming you'd be praying while doing these steps as well. That was also intentional, because it dovetails into the final Key for Effective Prayer.

7. Ain't Nothin' to It But to Do It!

"God helps those who help themselves." – Say what you will about the religion, the *Protestant Work Ethic* is spot on in describing reality.

Catholicism has a similar saying, variously ascribed to St. Augustine or St. Ignatius of Loyola: "We have to pray like it depends on God, but *work* like it depends on us!"

There's a massive spiritual truth in this, namely that the physical is a mirror image of the spiritual. The book of Hebrews alludes to this, when talking about the temple as "a sanctuary that is a copy and shadow of what is in heaven. This is why Moses was warned when he was about to build the tabernacle: 'See to it that you make everything according to the pattern shown you on the mountain.'" (Hebrews 8:5/NIV)

Hebrews 9:23 again talks about the "copies of the heavenly things," and traditionally the Catholic and Orthodox Churches both seek to order their worship after Biblical descriptions of how the Angels worship God in heaven.

The general principle here can be summarized as "*As above, so below. As below, so above*," and our application of the principle is that while our prayer that seeks to align the spiritual realms with our intentions, it's our work that does the same with the physical.
In essence, we seek to bring "that which is above" into harmony with "that which is below," insofar as both are in line with manifesting our intention.

The way this applies is that if you're looking for a job in your career field, you enhance this by filling out applications at any place that says "help wanted," no matter how menial. What this does is show you're serious about getting what you're praying for, and that you're willing to do whatever you have to do to make it happen. This also helps expand your sphere of availability (if you don't get the exact job you want, at least these others can be something to fall back on), and this is a display of sincerity and faith, which also translates into a display of loving the God to whom you're praying.

Another application of this is that if you want to make things happen in a subject about which you know nothing, start reading everything you can get your hands on. I once read that it takes reading 200 books to make someone an expert in any given subject, and I'm telling you those books, blog posts, and YouTube videos are going to start reading and watching themselves, just as your Sphere or Availability won't expand itself. Get to it!

Final Tips

In the end, these Seven Keys are a good starting point. Love God, yourself, and your neighbor; remember to be thankful; prayer involves not just your mouth but your entire being; and constantly work to expand your Sphere of Availability by doing everything you can in the physical world.

Praying in groups can also help you, as it ties love of God, Self, and Neighbor in one package. The bond of like-minded people praying for each others' intentions tends to manifest results faster than if a person is praying on their own. To this end you may want to look into joining a prayer group in your area, or talking with a few friends and forming on of your own.

In the beginning you may not see these Keys work out as well as you'd like, because it takes practice, constant self-examination, and perseverance. Just like we can't all be Slash the first time we pick up a guitar, we're not going to be prayer-masters the first time we pick up a Rosary, either.

"The prayer of the Rosary is perfect because of the praises it offers, the lessons it teaches, the graces it obtains, and the victories it achieves."

– Pope Benedict XV

8. The Expanded Rosary Method

Let's face it, this book is boring. If you've managed to keep your eyes open this far, though, that means either you have the patience of a Saint or you're actually learning something useful. My guess is that I'll know when you review this book on Amazon!

If you have made it this far, then we've covered a lot of ground together: the fundamentals of the Rosary, the spiritual implications of all 15 traditional Mysteries, the method for unlocking these Mysteries in your spiritual life, and the Seven Keys to making your prayer more effective. You'll also realize the whole point of this book is to turn your Rosary into a weapon.

On the bright side, you don't need to turn the Rosary into a weapon, because it already is one. On the not-so-bright side, just because you have a weapon doesn't mean you know how to use it. The steps I've shown you so far are a type of training intended to correct that.

With this in mind, the key to weaponizing the Rosary is found in the *Expanded Method*, a method I developed in 1998 and have used successfully ever since.

Roots of the Expanded Method

The expanded method has its roots in the "Second Method" given by St. Louis de Montfort in his *Secret of the Rosary*. I quote the Saint in his own words:

IN ORDER to do this [method] we must add a word or two to each Hail Mary (depending upon the decade) and this will help remind us which mystery we are commemorating. This word or words should be added after the word "Jesus." "And blessed is the fruit of Thy Womb";

At the 1st Decade . . . . . "Jesus incarnate;"
At the 2nd . . . . . "Jesus sanctifying;"
At the 3rd . . . . . "Jesus born in poverty;"
At the 4th . . . . . "Jesus sacrificed;"
At the 5th . . . . . "Jesus, Saint among Saints;"
At the 6th . . . . . "Jesus in His agony;"
At the 7th . . . . . "Jesus scourged;"
At the 8th . . . . . "Jesus crowned with thorns;"
At the 9th . . . . . "Jesus carrying His Cross;"
At the 10th . . . . . "Jesus crucified;"
At the 11th . . . . . "Jesus risen from the dead;"
At the 12th . . . . . "Jesus ascending to Heaven;"
At the 13th . . . . . "Jesus filling Thee with the Holy Spirit;"
At the 14th . . . . . "Jesus raising Thee up;"
At the 15th . . . . . "Jesus crowning Thee."

The next step in the evolution of this method can be seen in 1863, with Fr. Joseph Deharbe's *A Full Catechism of the Catholic Religion*. In this book Deharbe gives a number if inserts in the form of a "who" clause, for example "Jesus ... whom thou, O Virgin, didst conceive of the Holy Ghost." He tells us that, at the time of his writing, this was how the Rosary is recited in Germany (p. ix).

Enter my own practice. In the beginning, I turned this "who" clause into something that resonated more with me personally, that brought me more in touch with the main action of each Mystery. For example, in the Annunciation, I'd say "Jesus ... who was announced to thee by the Archangel Gabriel," or for the Scourging, "Jesus … who was scourged at the pillar," and so on. I've published the complete list in Latin and English my *We Pray the Rosary*, and for convenience will reprint the English here:

1. Annunciation … "who was announced to thee by the Archangel Gabriel."
2. Visitation … "who is the cause of our joy."
3. Nativity … "who was born in poverty."
4. Presentation … "who was presented in the temple."
5. Finding … "who confounded the doctors and priests in the temple."
6. Agony … "who sweated blood in Gethsemane."
7. Scourging … "who was scourged at the pillar."
8. Crowning … "who was crowned with cruel thorns."
9. Carrying … "who carried the cross for our sins."
10. Crucifixion … "who was crucified, died, and was buried for us."
11. Resurrection … "who on the third day rose again from the dead."
12. Ascension … "who ascended into heaven."
13. Pentecost … "who sent the Holy Ghost upon thee and upon his apostles."
14. Assumption … "who assumed thee into heaven."
15. Coronation … "who crowned thee Queen of Heaven and Empress of the Universe."

This change is what led to the Expanded Method, because rather than meditating on attributes of Jesus, the focus shifts to the *actions* of Jesus. With the new focus on the actions of Jesus comes a focus on the *actions of Jesus for you*.

The Expanded Method

The Expanded Method consists of simply meditating on the Mysteries as prescribed, while inserting the above clauses into the *Hail Mary* after the name of Jesus. Once all five decades, the *Salve Regina* and the Collect are completed, you add a final prayer:

O most Sorrowful and Immaculate Blessed Virgin Mary, Mother of God and Mother of men, thou who wast found worthy to carry God himself in thy womb, and thou who has crushed him who is at once the enemy of God and man in common under thy heel. Humbly do I, N., approach thee, through these Joyful (or Sorrowful, or Glorious) Mysteries of this thy Most Holy Rosary, asking that this offering may be acceptable to thee, and that thou wilt earnestly intercede on behalf of my petitions before the Father, namely that (here name your petitions). Through our Lord Jesus Christ thy Son, who with the Father liveth and reigneth in the unity of the Holy Ghost, God, forever and ever. Amen.

This prayer developed organically at the same time I developed the Expanded Method, and originally I would visualize the Blessed Mother in front of me and just talk out my problems and intentions by way of prayer. Eventually a formalized greeting evolved in my head and I started saying it, and after that a formalized conclusion. What you see here is the end result of this evolution.

9. Using the Rosary to Get Results

Thus far we've described the prayers, methods, and uses for the Rosary. Now we get into methods for getting results.

Expanded Method for Specific Intentions
The Expanded Method is excellent for bringing your intentions into manifestation, provided you make it a regular devotion (i.e. not only when you're asking for something) and practice the Seven Keys in addition to your Rosary. When there's something that you *really* need to manifest, then try the *Expanded Method for Specific Intentions*.

This is a slight variation on the Expanded Method, and functions by bringing your intentions into the Rosary itself. The variation is that instead of saying the Mystery's clause during the Hail Mary, you insert a different clause saying how Jesus made your intentions come to pass.

For example, if you're praying for a person to be proven innocent in court, you'd say "Jesus … who proved *(name)* innocent of all charges."

If you're looking for employment, you'd say, "Jesus … who found me work in *(my profession)*."

If you're looking for love, say, "Jesus … who brought true love into my life."

The variations are endless, and you should visualize your intention as though it had already come to pass. What this approach does is force your conscious mind's attention onto why you're really praying. In other words, it keeps you honest and doesn't allow you to hide behind false justifications of "I'm doing it for love of God" or other things people sometimes hide behind when saying their prayers.

What's the point of this? It's simple: honest prayer is much better at getting results, because it cuts through all the BS we tend to place between ourselves and God. By forcing yourself to be honest and direct about your reasons for doing this and not allowing yourself any room to feel guilt over it, you find yourself clearing a lot of mental and emotional hurdles out of the way.

When the Rosary is completed, conclude with the "*O Sorrowful and Immaculate*" prayer found in the Expanded Method.

Prayer Before a Rosary Novena

This seems a retooling of a classic prayer, though I've not been able to trace its history. It's used before saying the Rosary as a *Novena*, or nine days' prayer focused on a specific intention. Say it before your Rosary each day:

My dearest Mother Mary, behold me, your child, in prayer at your feet. Accept this Holy Rosary, which I offer you in accordance with your requests at Fatima, as a proof of my tender love for you, for the intentions of the Sacred Heart of Jesus, in atonement for the offenses committed against your Immaculate Heart, and for this special favor which I earnestly request in my Rosary Novena: (Mention your request).

I beg you to present my petition to your Divine Son. If you will pray for me, I cannot be refused. I know, dearest Mother, that you want me to seek God's holy Will concerning my request. If what I ask for should not be granted, pray that I may receive that which will be of greater benefit to my soul.

I offer you this spiritual "Bouquet of Roses" because I love you. I put all my confidence in you, since your prayers before God are most powerful. For the greater glory of God and for the sake of Jesus, your loving Son, hear and grant my prayer. Sweet Heart of Mary, be my salvation.

After saying this prayer, begin the Rosary as you normally would, while meditating on the Mysteries as appropriate to the day of the week. This can be used with the Basic or Expanded Rosary method, whichever you're accustomed to using in your daily practice.

Candles and the Rosary

If Catholics are known not only for the Rosary, but also for burning candles during prayer. The candles are a symbol of Christ's light going forth into the world, and the color of a candle (or the votive glass or "globe" into which it's put) represents a symbol either of the Saint to which – or the intention for which – we're praying.

This means candles can be used alongside the Rosary to help direct our minds and prayers, to help intensify our focus, and ideally so that this intensifies our prayer and therefore our results.

You can use any kind of candle for this purpose: tapers, tea lights, 7-day candles, and so forth. The candle can be white or the color associated with the patron Saint of your intention, or the color can be associated with your intention. When you light the candle, say a brief prayer in your own words, identifying your intention and showing confidence that it will be made manifest.

The colors associated with each Saint can be found on the internet, and here are the colors associated with each intention:

1. Red – love, blood, strength, vigor, or energy. As a vestment color it's worn on feasts of the Martyrs, of the Holy Cross, and the Holy Ghost.

2. Orange –healing, stimulation, or encouragement. Not a vestment color.

3. Yellow – joy, happiness, and confidence. Though no longer a vestment color, in the medieval Church this was the color of joy, worn on the feast-days of Confessors.

4. Green – hope, fertility, money, and growth. As a vestment Color it's worn during the time after Epiphany and the time after Pentecost, known on the post-Vatican II calendar as "Ordinary Time."

5. Blue – peace, devotion, meditation, protection, calming, and tranquility. Though not a "standard" vestment color, blue is considered the color of the Blessed Virgin Mary and permitted on her feast-days in Spanish-speaking countries.

Blue has historically been used as a vestment color for Advent in some liturgical Protestant churches (Swedish Lutheranism, for example), and is now considered the *de facto* Advent color within mainline American Protestantism.

6. Indigo *(interchangeable with black)* – tension, binding, depression, and death, release, and absorption of negativity. As a vestment color, black is the color of death and traditionally worn on Good Friday, the All Souls' Day, and at all funerals and Masses for the dead.

7. Violet – change, spiritual power, spirituality, purification, penance, and mourning. As a vestment color, it's during Advent and Lent, as well as during Ember Days and Rogations on the pre-Vatican II calendar.

8. White – purity, innocence, protection, and divine intervention. As a vestment color it's worn on all feasts of Our Lord, of the Blessed Virgin Mary, and of saints who are not martyrs.

If you're using seven-day candles, especially the cheap ones from the grocery store, then it's a good idea to put them in a loaf pan filled with sand while they burn. The reason is that sometimes the glass will crack, and the sand will catch the wax and help prevent your home from catching fire.

Let the candle burn while you pray your Rosary for the day. When your Rosary is finished, you may either put the candle out or leave it burning, depending on safety factors – you don't want to burn your house down – and what feels right to you.

The 54-Day Novena of Pompeii

While the Expanded Methods given above are sufficient for almost all needs, there are times when you might want to bring a lot of "umph" to bear in your situation. If you've got the self-discipline to go almost two months, then this 54-day Novena might come in handy.

This exercise is called the *Novena to Our Lady of Pompeii*, and is described in the English language by Charles V. Lacey, in his 1926 book *Rosary Novenas to Our Lady*:

> "In an apparition of Our Lady of Pompeii, which occurred in 1884 at Naples, in the house of Commander Agrelli, the heavenly Mother deigned to make known the manner in which she desires to be invoked.

> "For thirteen months Fortuna Agrelli, the daughter of he Commander, had endured dreadful sufferings and torturous cramps; she had been given up by the most celebrated physicians. On February 16, 1884, the afflicted girl and her relatives commenced a novena of Rosaries. The Queen of the Holy Rosary favored her with an

apparition on March 3rd. Mary, sitting upon a high throne, surrounded by luminous figures, held the Divine Child on her lap, and in her hand a Rosary. The Virgin Mother and the holy Infant were clad in gold-embroidered garments. They were accompanied by St. Dominic and St. Catherine of Siena. The throne was profusely decorated with flowers; the beauty of Our Lady was marvelous. The picture can be viewed on the previous page, just scroll down.

"Mary looked upon the sufferer with maternal tenderness, and the patient saluted her with the words: 'Queen of the Holy Rosary, be gracious to me; restore me to health! I have already prayed to thee in a novena, O Mary, but have not yet experienced thy aid. I am so anxious to be cured!'

"'Child,' responded the Blessed Virgin, 'thou hast invoked me by various titles and hast always obtained favors from me. Now, since thou hast called me by that title so pleasing to me, 'Queen of the Holy Rosary,' I can no longer refuse the favor thou dost petition; for this name is most precious and dear to me. Make three novenas, and thou shalt obtain all.'

"Once more the Queen of the Holy Rosary appeared to her and said, 'Whoever desires to obtain favors from me should make *three novenas of the prayers* of the Rosary, and *three novenas in thanksgiving.*'

"This miracle of the Rosary made a very deep impression on Pope Leo XIII, and greatly contributed to the fact that in so many circular letters he urged all Christians to love the Rosary and say it fervently."

Lacey is careful to tell us this story isn't supposed to be believed as a divine fact, but that "*no higher authority is claimed than that which is due to all authentic human testimony.*" He also attributes this story to a booklet titled *The Rosary, My Treasure*, by a Benedictine Convent in Clyde, Missouri. This booklet seems to have been published in several editions, and though I've not found the exact edition Lacey is quoting, I've managed to find an edition dated 1950 that contains the same Novena. It can be found at: https://archive.org/details/rosarymytreasure00bene_0.

Back to the Novena, its method consists of five decades of the Rosary each day for twenty-seven days in petition; then immediately five decades each day for twenty-seven days in thanksgiving, *whether or not the request has been granted*. On each day, we simply pray the Mysteries assigned to that day of the week, and there are no restrictions on whether to use the basic method, the Expanded Method, or any method of choice so long as the Mysteries and prayers are said in the right order.

Now for the fun part: how this Novena works. As with all good methods of prayer, this Novena's work is two-fold. Firstly, it develops personal discipline and requires a certainly of purpose to continue the entire 54 days, meaning the only way you're likely to continue it is by having no doubts or uncertainties that you really want what you're asking. Secondly, it creates a two-way current: upwards by way of petition, and downwards by way of thanksgiving.

While saying this Novena or any other, remember the Seven Keys to Effective Prayer, and constantly work to expand your Sphere of Availability.

REGINA SACRATISSIMI ROSARII, ORA PRO NOBIS

10. Final Considerations

We've done a lot of talking about origin, theory, and method. Now it's time to talk about things that can go wrong.

My Prayer Wasn't Answered

Sometimes, especially when you're just starting out, you may think your prayers aren't being answered. Most times, this isn't the case so much as the proverbial dominoes aren't in place for the desired result to occur.

Case in point, I remember a time after a brutal break-up when I wanted my girlfriend back. I used the Pompeii Novena to this effect and even got back on talking terms with her, but no reunion came to pass. However, three years later I met and became involved with a woman who looked like her and had pretty much the same personality. Let's analyze this for a minute.

The first thing to ask is why I didn't end up with my old girlfriend, even if I'd done everything right. It turns out I hadn't done everything right, which is why it didn't manifest.

For example, my reason for praying this (and I'm embarrassed to admit it) was a fear of loneliness and a feeling of possessiveness. These aren't the qualities of a person who loves himself, and in fact they can indicate an imbalance that can interfere with love of self, the Second Key to Effective Prayer. Possessiveness is also not synonymous with love of her, which extends broadly into the category of Love of Neighbor, the Third Key.

Another issue was my Sphere of Availability. I've always been socially awkward, for example, and didn't have anything in the way of "game." In fact I still don't, but at the time I was more attractive than I am now. She'd also started seeing someone else and – what I didn't know at the time – had become pregnant with his child. I say this without commenting on the morality of the situation, but merely to report the events as they happened; what happened is that this combination of events, along with our prior relationship ending badly, moved her far out of my Sphere of Availability. The Sixth Key, in other words, was lacking.

Okay, so we can see what went wrong here. So what about the woman who showed up three years later? Let's talk about her, since she represents something interesting.

Three years after the break-up, I was somewhat more secure as a person and had developed at least a little more social skills (I say "a little," because anybody watching my YouTube videos can tell I'm still awkward). This new woman and I also had no previous history, leaving a greater openness to whatever sort of affinity. In other words, the issues with Keys Two and Three weren't there, at least in this case, and my Sphere of Availability had expanded accordingly.

The other interesting point is the time. Why did it take three years? This demonstrates three things, first that prayers left at God's throne can find themselves answered even if long-forgotten by the person praying them; second that a prayer may wait until the surrounding circumstances become more favorable; and third that prayers can find themselves answered more effortlessly if you stop wanting something so badly.

One final interesting thing in this connection is that it showed me *why* the prayer would've been better left unanswered. Let's just say this new woman and I weren't exactly a good match; the similarities in their personalities taught me that my and I wouldn't have been a good match either. A few years later I was approached by an investigator working for a divorce lawyer; the lawyer was hired by the man by whom my ex had become pregnant (they had since married), and the man and I finally met face-to-face.

The stories I heard at that meeting (all of which were proven true) convinced me that any prayer I'd uttered regarding said ex-girlfriend was better off unheeded. I've come to believe this "blockage" of results can also be a function of our subconscious protecting us from something it knows is bad for us. The traditional explanation is that "God knows when something's not good for us," and I've come to believe we instinctively know when something's not good for us, either.

Results Are Taking Too Long!

This depends on your definition of "too long." Consider that the founder of Pandora was turned down by 300 investors before finding one who'd fund this startup. Or consider that James Dyson created 5,127 failed prototypes for a bagless vacuum cleaner.

We're talking about a lot of let-down here, but what did they do? *They kept trying.*

After 300 rejections by investors, investor #301 said "Let's make this happen." After 5,127 failed prototypes, prototype #5,128 got the job done. The lesson from this is *failure sucks, but instructs*. The other lesson is that *we need to keep on truckin'*.

If you feel your results are taking too long, it could be that something is in the way of manifesting them. Usually this stems from whether you actually want what you're asking, or (more often) because your Sphere of Availability isn't where it needs to be just yet.

Take a moment to examine your situation as unemotionally and dispassionately as possible, and look to find out what skill set you might need to develop, or whether you need to more people's eyeballs looking at any public part of what you're doing. Find out what obstacles exist in the way of your intention and how best they can be overcome, and any areas where you're Sphere is too contracted to manifest what you're looking for *right now*. And most importantly, *keep at it*.

I think one example of this is David Bawden. Most people laugh at him, because he calls himself "Pope Michael I of the Roman Catholic Church;" the story behind this is long, but what happened is that his parents and four other people declared him Pope in 1990. Ever since the internet was invented he had a website and some sort of outreach, but very few people would accept him as their pontiff; as of 2010, all that changed and while his following is still small, he does have an actual following.

Now people might laugh at Bawden and everything he represents – I don't exactly support him and am not writing to condemn – but he illustrates why perseverance is so important. He and his mother prayed hard to make something happen, and after 20 years of nothing, finally the dam burst and people started coming to him.

Part of what happened were advances in technology; it was hard to reach out from a small town in Kansas, until the internet, YouTube, and Facebook brought the world closer together. Even with the internet, competition for eyeballs is fierce, but other people with their own audiences started taking note of Bawden, first by writing about him in *What's the Matter with Kansas* and then with the *Pope Michael* documentary uploaded to Vimeo in 2010. In essence, his Sphere of Availability was too small and it took 20 years to expand it.

No matter what you think of Pope Michael, you can learn from him. You can learn the importance of sticking with it in the face of seemingly insurmountable odds, and the importance of constantly seeking to expand your Sphere.

I'm Getting Side-Effects!

I remember one time I helped a friend. She'd asked me to help her friend find a romantic partner. I obliged, it worked, but for the next two months women were literally throwing themselves at me. This is something called a *side-effect*.

A side-effect happens when you put too much of yourself into your prayer, or your Sphere of Availability happens to be in the really right for whatever it is you're praying. Even so, it's not always a good thing.

Case in point, the example of women throwing themselves at me. Being a straight guy and most of these women being attractive, I thought it was awesome. But what if one of those women were married to an overly jealous husband? She so much as says "hi" to me and I get my head blown off, would that be awesome? *Even if we think the side-effects are good, we should always seek to avoid them.*

The good news is that with time, you'll learn to avoid side-effects the same way a beginning driver learns how to control his foot-pressure on the gas pedal. It takes practice, and in time you'll get there.

Closing Thoughts

With time and practice, you'll learn how to discern if a prayer's being blocked, if your Sphere needs to expand, or if there's a personality trait within yourself that's hindering manifestation. You'll learn to tell whether you really want what you're asking, or if it's better to pick up your marbles and go home. Don't let yourself become disheartened at any step of the way, and with patience and perseverance you, too, will learn to wield the Rosary as the finely-tuned instrument and deadly-edged weapon it was meant to be.

Appendix A. Mysteries and Days of the Week

1. Traditional Mysteries
Monday – Joyful
Tuesday – Sorrowful
Wednesday – Glorious
Thursday – Joyful
Friday – Sorrowful
Saturday – Glorious

Sundays from Advent to Lent – Joyful
Sundays from Lent to Easter – Sorrowful
Sundays from Easter Sunday to Advent – Glorious

2. With the Luminous Mysteries
Monday – Joyful
Tuesday – Sorrowful
Wednesday – Glorious
Thursday – Luminous
Friday – Joyful
Saturday – Sorrowful
Sunday – Glorious

Appendix B. Rosary Prayers in Latin

Sign of the Cross
In nómine Patris, et Fílii, et Spíritus Sancti. Amen.

Apostles' Creed
Credo in Deum Patrem omnipoténtem, Creatórem cæli et terræ. Et in Jesum Christum, Fílium ejus únicum, Dóminum nostrum, qui concéptus est de Spíritu Sancto, natus ex María Vírgine, passus sub Póntio Piláto, crucifíxus, mórtuus, et sepúltus, descéndit ad ínferos, tértia die resurréxit a mórtuis, ascéndit ad cælos, sedet ad déxteram Dei Patris omnipoténtis, inde ventúrus est judicáre vivos et mórtuos. Credo in Spíritum Sanctum, sanctam Ecclésiam cathólicam, sanctórum communiónem, remissiónem peccatórum, carnis resurrectiónem, vitam ætérnam. Amen.

Our Father
Pater noster, qui es in caelis: sanctificétur nomen tuum; advéniat regnum tuum; fiat volúntas tua, sicut in caelo, et in terra. Panem nostrum quotidiánum da nobis hódie; et dimítte nobis débita nostra, sicut et nos dimíttimus debitóribus nostris: et ne nos indúcas in tentatiónem; sed líbera nos a malo.
Lord's Prayer Doxology or "Protestant Ending"
Quia tuum est regnum, et potéstas, et glória, in sǽcula. Amen.

Hail Mary – Catholic
Ave María, grátia plena, Dóminus tecum. Benedícta tu in muliéribus, et benedíctus fructus ventris tui, Jesus. Sancta María, Mater Dei, ora pro nobis peccatóribus, nunc et in hora mortis nostræ. Amen.

Hail Mary – Protestant
Ave María, grátia plena, Dóminus tecum. Benedícta tu in muliéribus, et benedíctus fructus ventris tui, Jesus Christus. Amen.

Glory Be to the Father
Glória Patri, et Fílio, et Spirítui Sancto. Sicut erat in princípio, et nunc, et semper, et in sǽcula sæculórum. Amen.

Fatima Prayer (Optional)
O mi Jesu, dimítte nobis débita nostra, líbera nos ab igne inférni, conduc in cælum omnes animas, præsértim illas, quæ máxime indigent misericórdia tua. Amen.

Hail, Holy Queen and Collect
Salve, Regína, mater misericórdiæ, vita, dulcédo, et spes nostra, salve. Ad te clamámus éxsules fílii Hevæ. Ad te suspirámus, geméntes et flentes in hac lacrimárum valle. Eja, ergo, advocáta nostra, illos tuos misericórdes óculos ad nos convérte. Et Jesum, benedíctum fructum ventris tui, nobis post hoc exsílium osténde. O clemens, O pia, O dulcis Virgo María.

V. Regína sacratíssimi Rosárii, ora pro nobis.
R. Ut digni efficiámur promissiónibus Christi.

Orémus. Deus, cujus Unigénitus per vitam, mortem et resurrectiónem suam nobis salútis ætérnæ præmia comparávit, concéde, quæsumus: ut hæc mystéria sacratíssimo beátæ Maríæ Vírginis Rosário recoléntes, et imitémur quod cóntinent, et quod promíttunt assequámur. Per eúndem Christum Dóminum nostrum. Amen.

Magnificat (Lutheran Rosary)

Magníficat * ánima mea Dóminum.

Et exultávit spíritus meus: * in Deo salutári meo.

Quia respéxit humilitátem ancíllae suae:* Ecce enim ex hoc beátam me dicent omnes generatiónes.

Quia fécit mihi mágna qui pótens est: * et sánctum nómen eius.

Et misericórdia ejus in progénies et progénies * timéntibus eum.

Fécit poténtiam in bráchio suo: * dispérsit supérbos mente cordis sui.

Depósuit poténtes de sede: * et exaltávit húmiles.

Esuriéntes implévit bonis: * et dívites dimísit inánes.

Suscépit Israël púerum suum: * recordátus misericórdiæ suæ.

Sicut locútus est ad patres nostros: * Abraham, et sémini ejus in sǽcula.

Glória Patri, et Fílio, et Spirítui Sancto, * Sicut erat in princípio, et nunc, et semper, et in sǽcula sæculórum. Amen.

Appendix C. Intentions for Each Mystery

1. Annunciation:
Learning the virtue of humility, discerning or strengths and shortcomings, finding ways toward new beginnings, speeding our intentions into manifestation.

2. Visitation:
Learning the virtue of charity, manifesting prayers involving love, family, and relationships, business associations, romantic partnerships, awareness of the interconnections of all life.

3. Nativity:
Learning detachment without falling into derangement, learning to focusing one's mind without becoming distracted, hastening the physical manifestation of necessities (money, food, etc.) to sustain one's current physical condition, seeing what needs to be done in getting out of unfavorable situations, and working ourselves into a position where we have more control over our lives.

4. Presentation:
Learning obedience to divine law, learning and application of the natural and social sciences, engineering, mechanical work, and so forth. By extension this Mystery can help us in matters of human law, authority relationships, and matters involving ethical or moral decisions.

5. Finding in the Temple:

Conversion to a deeper following of Christ, breaking away of ignorance in ourselves and others, opening our eyes to realize our proverbial "blind spots" and options for self-improvement, overcoming and/or healing our weaknesses (physical, mental, emotional), and for helping others come around to see our point of view.

6. Agony in the Garden:

Discovering and overcoming our own problems, confronting deep-seated issues keeping us from reaching our full potential, giving us courage to start a new task, overcoming competition or lawsuits when our cause is just, overcoming trust issues in ourselves and others, and finding the courage and energy to realize our full potential.

7. Scourging:

Gaining control over physical urges (sex, overeating, etc.), getting an unreciprocated admirer to back off, ending relationships that have gone on "past their expiration date," finding one's way out of an abusive situation.

8. Crowning with Thorns:

Learning to control our minds and emotions, finding peace within oneself, establishing peace within a community, encouraging people to work past their differences and objects of contention to cooperate as far as possible.

9. Carrying the Cross:

The virtue of perseverance, the strength and willpower to keep at something, patience, the will to see a project through to completion, empowerment in the ability to persevere. This Mystery can be useful especially to spiritual novices and entrepreneurs, and others whose goals involve sticking it out through long-range planning.

10. Crucifixion:
Letting go of our old selves, bringing an end to bad or no-longer-necessary circumstances in our lives, manifesting forgiveness as proper and necessary, and emptying out the old to make way for the new.

11. Resurrection:
Learning to defend one's faith (apologetics), protecting loved ones from being evangelized by people who want them to abandon their own beliefs, gaining constancy of will and works of renewal after a massive loss or a bad downturn, whether this renewal is needed in the sphere of love, business, health, or any other area of life.

12. Ascension:
Bringing into one's life an abundance of clarity and hope, gaining a big-picture view on a deeper level, best worked in conjunction with the Nativity and the Scourging.

13. Descent of the Holy Ghost:
Bringing about a heavy influx of Divine Power, Divine Love, understanding, self-transformation, can be useful in work involving social issues.

14. Assumption (Communion of Saints):
Bringing a work towards its completion, protecting the work until it is completed, helping and applying our earned indulgences to deceased loved ones and the Poor Souls in Purgatory.

15. Coronation (Heavenly Jerusalem):

Manifesting justice, revealing those falsely accused and guilty parties who've been overlooked, establishing unity towards completing a purpose This Mystery can also be appealed in conjunction with the others to lend extra blessing to the work at hand.

Hic Est Enim Finis Libri Nostri. Ite, Mi Amici, et Prosperate!

Other Books by THAVMA Publications

The Magic of Catholicism: Real Magic for Devout Catholics

The Vatican II Rite of Exorcism: the Complete 1999 Ritual

Is Magic Wrong?
(get this for free at http://thavmapub.com)

Ritual Magic for Conservative Christians

We Pray the Rosary

The Magic of Effective Prayer

Christian Spiritual and Magical Rituals

Guide to Meditation

Christian Candle Magic

Made in United States
North Haven, CT
26 April 2024

51812414R00065